Bible Story Basics: Scope & Sequence

Year 1: Fall	Year 1: Winter	Year 1: Spring	Year 1: Summer	Year 2: Fall
UNIT 1: Beginnings Genesis 1:31	**UNIT 1: Hope** Isaiah 2:5	**UNIT 1: Journey** Psalm 121:8	**UNIT 1: Paul** Philippians 4:13	**UNIT 1: Joseph** Jeremiah 29:11
1. Creation — Genesis 1:1-25	1. Swords into Plows — Isaiah 2:1-5	1. Man in the Synagogue — Matthew 12:9-14	1. Paul's Conversion — Acts 9:1-20	1. Joseph and His Brothers — Genesis 37:1-36
2. God's Image — Genesis 1:26–2:4a	2. Mary's Story — Luke 1:26-38, 46-47	2. Jesus and the Children — Matthew 19:13-15	2. Love in Action — Romans 12:9-18	2. Joseph in Egypt — Genesis 39:1–40:23
3. Adam and Eve — Genesis 2:4b–3:24	3. Joseph's Story — Matthew 1:18-24	3. Last Supper — Matthew 26:17-30	3. Paul Escapes — Acts 9:20-25	3. Joseph Saves the Day — Genesis 41:1-57
4. Noah — Genesis 6:1–9:17	4. Jesus' Story — Luke 2:1-7	4. In the Garden — Matthew 26:31-56	4. Be Glad and Endure — Philippians 4:4-14	4. Joseph and His Brothers Reunite — Genesis 42:1–46:34
5. Tower of Babel — Genesis 11:1-9	5. Shepherds' Story — Luke 2:8-20	5. Peter — Matthew 26:57-58, 69-75		
UNIT 2: Ancestors Genesis 15:5	**UNIT 2: Calling** Matthew 4:19	**UNIT 2: Alleluia** Matthew 28:7	**UNIT 2: Leaders** 2 Timothy 1:7	**UNIT 2: Exodus** Exodus 3:12
6. Abraham and Sarah — Genesis 12:1-9; 15:1-6	6. Follow the Star — Matthew 2:1-12	6. Hosanna! — Matthew 21:1-11; 27:32-66	5. Timothy Is Chosen — Acts 16:1-5; 1 Timothy 4:7b-16	5. The Baby in the Basket — Exodus 1:8–2:10
7. Abraham and Lot — Genesis 13:1-12	7. Jesus Is Baptized — Matthew 3:13-17	7. Easter — Matthew 28:1-10	6. Be Encouraged — Timothy 1:3-7	6. The Burning Bush — Exodus 2:11–3:22
8. The Birth of Isaac — Genesis 18:1-15; 21:1-7	8. Jesus Calls the Fishermen — Matthew 4:18-22	8. Breakfast on the Beach — John 21:1-19	7. Lydia — Acts 16:11-15	7. Moses and Pharaoh — Exodus 5:1–13:9
9. Isaac and Rebekah — Genesis 24:1-67	9. Beatitudes — Matthew 5:1-12	9. The Great Commission — Matthew 28:16-20	8. Paul and Silas — Acts 16:16-40	8. Crossing the Sea — Exodus 13:17–14:31
UNIT 3: Blessings Genesis 28:14	**UNIT 3: Wisdom** Matthew 7:24	**UNIT 3: Believers** Acts 2:4	**UNIT 3: Prophets** 1 Kings 18:39	**UNIT 2: Wilderness** Exodus 15:2
10. Jacob and Esau — Genesis 25:19-28	10. The Lord's Prayer — Matthew 6:5-15	10. Believers Share — Acts 4:32-37	9. Elijah and the Ravens — 1 Kings 16:29-30; 17:1-7	9. Songs of Joy — Exodus 15:1-21
11. The Birthright — Genesis 25:29-34	11. The Birds in the Sky — Matthew 6:25-34	11. Choosing the Seven — Acts 6:1-7	10. Elijah and the Prophets — 1 Kings 18:20-39	10. In the Wilderness — Exodus 15:22–17:7
12. The Blessing — Genesis 27:1-46	12. The Golden Rule — Matthew 7:12	12. Philip and the Ethiopian — Acts 8:26-40	11. Elijah and Elisha — 1 Kings 19:1-21	11. Ten Commandments — Exodus 19:1–20:21
13. Jacob's Dream — Genesis 28:10-22	13. The Two Houses — Matthew 7:24-27	13. First Called "Christians" — Acts 11:19-30	12. Elisha and the Widow — 2 Kings 4:1-7	12. A House for God — Exodus 25:1–31:18; 35:4–40:38
		14. Pentecost — Acts 2:1-41	13. Elisha and Naaman — 2 Kings 5:1-19a	13. Elizabeth and Zechariah — Luke 1:5-25

Contents

- 2 Welcome to Bible Story Basics
- 3 What Children Ages 3-7 Need
- 4 Using This Leader Guide
- 5 Resources
- 6 Supplies

UNIT 1: Hope
- 7 **Session 1**
  Swords into Plows
- 13 **Session 2**
  Mary's Story
- 19 **Session 3**
  Joseph's Story
- 25 **Session 4**
  Jesus' Story
- 31 **Session 5**
  Shepherds' Story

UNIT 2: Calling
- 37 **Session 6**
  Follow the Star
- 43 **Session 7**
  Jesus Is Baptized
- 49 **Session 8**
  Jesus Calls the Fishermen
- 55 **Session 9**
  Beatitudes

UNIT 3: Wisdom
- 61 **Session 10**
  The Lord's Prayer
- 67 **Session 11**
  The Birds in the Sky
- 73 **Session 12**
  The Golden Rule
- 79 **Session 13**
  The Two Houses

Supplemental Pages
- 85 Song Lyrics
- 87 Bible Verse Signs
- 90 Additional Reproducibles
- 96 Comments from Users

Bible STORY BASICS

- unleashes the power of God's Word to work in the minds and hearts of children;
- establishes the Bible as foundational in children's lives and faith;
- equips both leaders and children to read, appreciate, and understand Scripture and its historical context and enduring message; and
- provides children a depth of spiritual resources to draw upon in difficult times.

Check out
www.biblestorybasics.com
to stay up to date on all the
Bible Story Basics news.

Written by Daphna Flegal.
Cover design by Ed Maksimowicz. Illustrations by Ralph Voltz.

Art—p. 2: Ralph Voltz; pp. 6, 18, 42, 54, 60, 66, 72, 78, 90, 91, 93, 94: Four Story Creative, Thinkstock, Shutterstock®, Cokesbury curriculum, and Abingdon curriculum; p. 12: Nathalie Beauvois/Deborah Wolfe, Ltd.; pp. 24, 48: Craig Cameron/Deborah Wolfe, Ltd.; p. 30: Robbie Short; p. 36: Glenn Zimmer/Wendy Lynn; p. 84: Robert S. Jones; pp. 87, 88, 89: Diana Magnuson.

Welcome to

We're glad you're here! This year you and your kids will journey together to discover tools for reading and learning the Bible. Your children will hear foundational Bible stories, memorize key verses, and internalize God's Word while having fun with music, games, puzzles, prayer, and more!

Bible Story Basics is a comprehensive three-year Bible study built to help children understand the overarching story of God's Word while nurturing and growing their faith—without a lot of complicated extras.

With a simple look and feel, these lessons are straightforward and easy to teach. The broad age-level structure (ages 3-7 and 8-12) makes it simple to group your children, while also providing leaders the confidence to teach age-appropriate lessons.

We invite you and your children to experience the depths of God's love expressed in the stories of the Bible. It's basic!

What Children Ages 3-7 Need

For developing faith foundations, children need	For knowing the Bible and our faith traditions, children need	For relating to God and the church, children need	For relating faith to daily living, children need
• to be with adults whose Christian attitudes and behaviors the children can imitate; • to have their feelings and actions accepted and to be forgiven when they do not meet adult expectations; • to develop and express their own identity as individuals and in relation to others; • to be guided in playing cooperatively with other children; and • to practice decision-making through optional activities.	• to handle the Bible and see others read from it; • to sing and say Bible verses, especially from Psalms and the Gospels; • to recognize the Lord's Prayer, the Golden Rule, and other affirmations of our faith; • to hear stories of Bible people who lived as God wanted them to live; • to participate in Communion with parents or other caregivers; and • to hear short stories about the church today and in the past.	• to learn simple prayers; • to be encouraged to give their own offerings to God and to the church; • to develop a sense of belonging at church and of being a child of God; • to have accepting adults who are willing to hear their many questions about God, life, death, and crises; and • to experience awe and wonder through nature, life cycles, and corporate worship, even though they may not be able to talk about the meanings of their experiences.	• to hear stories about service to others and to observe leaders, parents, and older children in service to others; • to participate in service by making things for others and by sharing money and food; • to hear leaders, parents, or guardians pray about people and situations beyond themselves; • to use Sunday school take-home items as reminders of what they learned in Sunday school; and • to practice caring for and appreciating God's world.

Using This Leader Guide

Underlying each aspect of the Bible Story Basics curriculum is the belief that all children should have the opportunity to experience the depths of God's love for them expressed in the timeless stories of the Bible. Each story-focused session allows the narrative to drive children's faith formation and provides a rich context for the development of biblical literacy skills.

Bible Background and Devotion

The first page of each Leader Guide session offers Bible background and a devotion to help the facilitator prepare for the lesson, better understand the biblical context, and spend a few moments in meditation and prayer.

Lesson Flow

B - The flow of the lesson starts with **Bible Beginnings**. This is the time to welcome the children and introduce the Bible story. Each week, the pre-readers will have a coloring picture of the Bible story and a Bible puzzle. There is also a suggestion for Bible play. Play is an important way young children learn. This activity will focus their play on the Bible story.

I - The lesson then moves **Into the Bible**. This will include two opportunities for the children to hear the Bible story, one from the Bible Basics Storybook and one from the week's Bible Story Leaflet. The leaflet story will be interactive. This section will also include the Bible tool, helping the children learn the Bible verse and the mechanics of the Bible.

B - Following the Bible story, the children will experience activities that help them make **Bible Connections**. These activities draw from various learning styles to present age-appropriate ideas and help deepen the children's understanding of the Bible story.

L - Next, the lesson moves to activities that will help the children **Live the Bible** and make the Bible relevant to their own lives.

E - Finally, the lesson will close with opportunities to **Express Praise**. This section includes a song and prayer, plus suggestions for how you can bless and affirm each child.

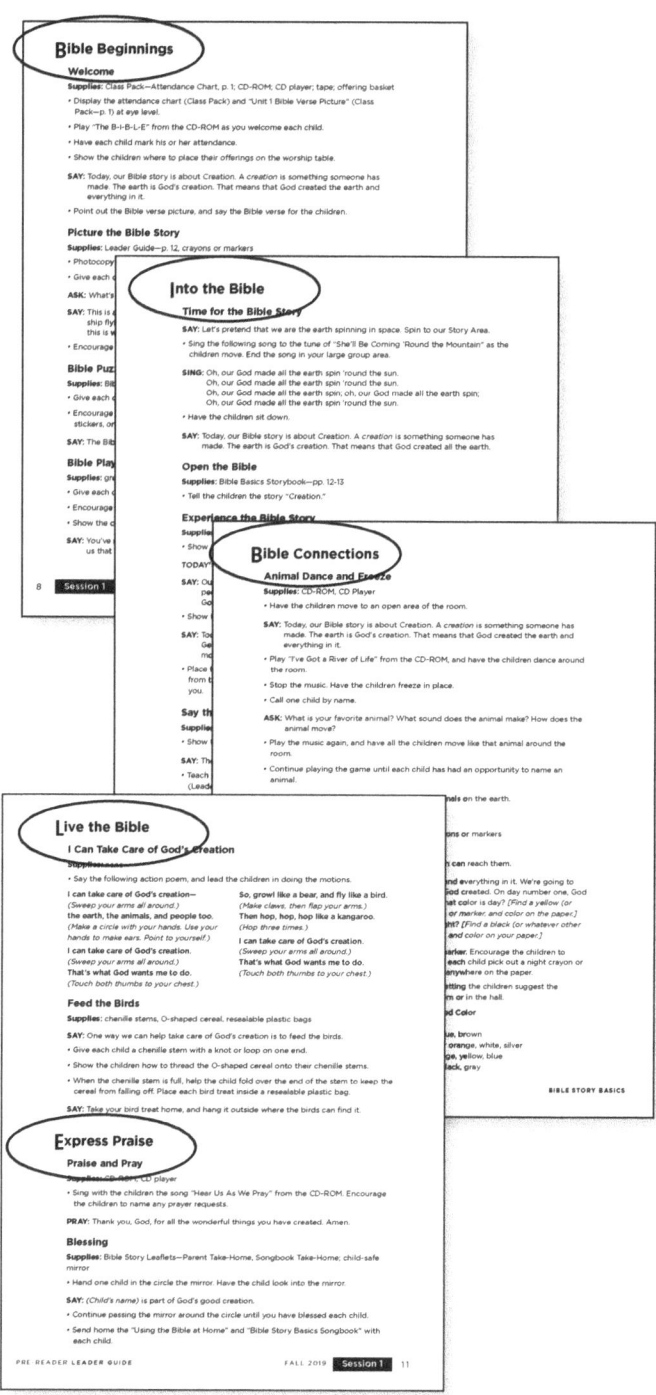

Resources

Leader Guide
This guide features 13 low-prep and step-by-step session guides that offer creative ways for children to experience foundational Bible stories through a variety of learning styles.

Bible Story Leaflets
These leaflets feature colorful and realistic art from Ralph Voltz and offer creative ways to involve children in the Bible story and to facilitate a connection between church and home with weekly questions and prayers to share as a family.

Class Pack
The annual Class Pack includes 12 Bible verse pictures to assist in Scripture memorization, a CD-ROM containing music and additional teaching materials, and an attendance chart. The additional teaching materials on the CD-ROM are also available to download at *biblestorybasics.com/resources*.

Student Take-Home CD
This CD includes seven memorable songs for the children to learn and enjoy throughout the year. The CD is sold in packs of five at a price that makes it possible to send one home with each child.

Bible Basics Storybook
The 149 Old and New Testament stories in this storybook will invite your child into the Word through beautiful illustrations, retellings that are appropriate for young children, and prayers that connect to our faith.

Bible Story Basics resources are available in Braille on request.

Contact:
Braille Ministry
c/o Donna Veigel
10810 N. 91st Avenue #96
Peoria, AZ 85345
(623)-979-7552

Supplies

No matter what activities you choose to use, there are some basic supplies you likely will need at some point. Collect these supplies and keep them accessible every Sunday.

The Basics
- baby dolls
- CD player
- CEB Bibles
- chenille stems
- child-safe mirror
- construction paper
- craft sticks
- crayons
- flashlight
- glue
- hole punch
- interlocking blocks or wood blocks
- markers
- nonbreakable Nativity set
- offering basket
- paintbrushes
- paint smocks
- paper plates
- plain paper
- plastic table covering
- ribbon
- scissors
- stickers
- tape
- tissue paper
- towels
- watercolor paint
- water table or plastic tub
- yarn

Beyond the Basics

Once you have chosen the activities in each session that you intend to do, check the specific supplies for each activity.

If some of the necessary supplies are slightly out of the ordinary, make a wish list of the supplies you will need. Publish the list in the church newsletter or bulletin. Members of your church will be happy to know how they can support the children in the church.

If you have a place to store supplies, encourage the congregation to bring the supplies you will need for the rest of the quarter. If you do not have a place to store things, make a new list each week of the things you will need in the next two or three weeks.

Swords into Plows

Bible Verse: Let's walk by the Lord's light. (Isaiah 2:5)

Bible Story: Isaiah 2:1-5

Bible Background

The Book of Isaiah takes its name from the prophet Isaiah of Jerusalem. God sent the prophets to particular places and times to speak God's Word to the people. Prophets didn't make predictions; they made observations about what is and what can be. They affirmed that the reign of God will bring about radical changes in the world.

Isaiah was born in the eighth century BC and probably lived into the early seventh century BC. He understood God primarily as the ruler of the universe, a ruler who has a plan for all creation. Isaiah 2:1-5, a well-known prophecy of peace, describes the world when the people will follow God's law. It's a beautiful image of peace. Nations will resolve their conflicts and unite in peace. Peace will run so deep, in fact, that the people won't have any need for weapons, so they will make their swords and spears into farm implements. They will participate in and respond to God's work in the world by shifting their attention from protecting themselves to producing abundance.

The image of beating swords into plows in Isaiah 2:4 may refer to breaking up a sword to make the metal tip of a plow. This tip breaks up the dirt and makes a furrow, allowing seeds to be planted. Likewise, spears will be transformed into pruning tools used to cut leaves and new shoots from grapevines, promoting new growth. Ancient samples indicate that these tools had a sharp, curved hook at the end, much like a sickle.

When we read Isaiah today, we see a God who demands justice for humankind. God finds a way, despite our resistance, to make the world just. Isaiah's message to us is a message of hope, echoed in our Advent celebrations and traditions.

Devotion

Look at the image of the bronze statue "Let Us Beat Swords into Ploughshares," created by Soviet artist Evgeniy Vuchetich. The statue was presented to the United Nations by the USSR in 1959. The sculpture is meant to symbolize our desire to put an end to war and convert the means of destruction into creative tools for the benefit of humankind. It is located in the garden at the headquarters of the United Nations. Read Isaiah 2:1-5. How can you work for peace?

biblestorybasics.com

BASIC

Plan

Bible Beginnings
Welcome
Picture the Bible Story
Bible Puzzle
Bible Play

Into the Bible
Time for the Bible Story
Open the Bible
Experience the Bible Story
Say the Bible Verse

Bible Connections
Make Bible Story Pictures
Flashlight Freeze

Live the Bible
Scroll Ornaments
Night Lights

Express Praise
Praise and Pray
Blessing

Bible Beginnings

Welcome

Supplies: Class Pack—Attendance Chart, p. 4; CD-ROM; CD player; tape; offering basket

- Display the attendance chart (Class Pack) and "Unit 1 Bible Verse Picture" (Class Pack—p. 4) at the children's eye level.
- Play "The B-I-B-L-E" from the CD-ROM (lyrics on p. 85) as you welcome each child.
- Have each child mark his or her attendance.
- Show the children where to place their offerings on the worship table.

SAY: In our Bible story today, we will hear words from a prophet named Isaiah. A prophet is someone who tells people how God wants us to live.

- Point out the Bible verse picture, and say the Bible verse for the children.

Picture the Bible Story

Supplies: Leader Guide—p. 12, crayons or markers

- Photocopy "Isaiah" for each child. Give each child the picture.

SAY: This is the prophet Isaiah. A prophet is someone who tells people how God wants us to live. Isaiah told people about God's plan for peace.

- Encourage the children to decorate the picture with crayons or markers.

Bible Puzzle

Supplies: Bible Story Leaflets—Session 1, p. 4; crayons or markers

- Give each child a copy of today's Bible Story Leaflet.

SAY: This is a picture of a Bible-times plow. Plows are used to dig up dirt so seeds can be planted. The prophet Isaiah talked about plows in our Bible story.

Bible Play

Supplies: plastic tray or box lid, clean sand or dirt, craft sticks

- Spread sand or dirt in the bottom of a plastic tray or box lid. Show the children how to use one end of a craft stick to make deep lines in the sand or dirt.

SAY: Let's pretend our craft sticks are plows. Use the sticks to make lines in the *(sand or dirt)*. In Bible times, a farmer used a plow to dig up the dirt and to make deep lines called furrows. Then the farmer scattered seeds in the furrows. The seeds grew into plants. The prophet Isaiah talked about plows in our Bible story.

Into the Bible

Time for the Bible Story

SAY: Let's walk to our Story Area.

- Sing the following song to the tune of "Row, Row, Row Your Boat" as the children move. End the song in your Story Area.

SING: Let's walk by the light.
Let's walk by the light.
Joyfully, joyfully, joyfully, joyfully,
Let's walk by the light.

- Sing the song again, changing how the children move. (For example, sing, "Let's hop by the light," "Let's stomp by the light," or "Let's march by the light.") Continue singing and changing the suggested movement as time and interest allow.

- Have the children sit down.

SAY: In our Bible story today, we will hear words from a prophet named Isaiah. A prophet is someone who tells people how God wants us to live. Isaiah said, "Let's walk by the Lord's light" (Isaiah 2:5).

Open the Bible

Supplies: Bible Basics Storybook—pp. 120-121

- Tell the children the story "Swords into Plows."

Experience the Bible Story

Supplies: CEB Bible; Bible Story Leaflets—Session 1, pp. 2-3

- Show the children the Bible.

TODAY'S BIBLE TOOL: The books about prophets are in the Old Testament.

SAY: A prophet is someone who tells people what God says. The books about prophets are in the Old Testament.

- Show the children the Book of Isaiah.

SAY: Today, our story is something that a prophet named Isaiah told the people.

- Place the leaflet inside the Bible. Tell the children the story "Swords into Plows" from the leaflet, and encourage them to lie or sit quietly with their eyes closed.

SAY: Isaiah told people about God's plan for peace. His words gave people hope. As Christians, we believe that Jesus is part of God's plan for peace and that knowing Jesus gives us hope.

ASK: What are some things you can do to live peacefully with your family? your friends?

Say the Bible Verse

Supplies: Class Pack—p. 4, Leader Guide—p. 87

- Show the children the Bible verse picture (Class Pack). Repeat the verse.

- Teach the children signs in American Sign Language to go along with the verse (Leader Guide).

- Encourage the children to make the signs as they say the verse again.

Bible Connections

Make Bible Story Pictures

Supplies: construction paper, craft sticks, glue, aluminum foil, optional: seeds

SAY: The prophet Isaiah said that a time is coming when there won't be any war. We won't need any weapons, such as swords. People will make swords into plows and other tools for planting seeds. Let's make a picture of a plow.

- Give each child a piece of construction paper and two craft sticks.
- Show the children how to glue the craft sticks in a V shape on their paper.

SAY: These sticks will make the handles of your plow.

- Use aluminum foil to make a sword.
- Show the children the foil sword. Tear off a piece of the foil sword for each child.

SAY: Let's pretend your foil is the point of a sword. Let's use the point to make the sharp blade of your plow.

- Have each child glue his or her foil piece at the point where the two craft sticks touch to add a blade to the plow.

SAY: Now, instead of a sword, we have plows. Farmers push plows on the dirt to make deep lines, or furrows, in the dirt. Then the farmers scatter seeds in the furrows.

- If you've provided seeds, let the children glue seeds around their plow.

Flashlight Freeze

Supplies: CD-ROM, CD player, flashlight

- Have the children move to an open area of the room.

SAY: The prophet Isaiah said, "Let's walk by the Lord's light" (Isaiah 2:5). Let's play a game with light. When you hear the music playing, start dancing. I'm going to move around you. When I shine the flashlight, everybody will freeze. Then let's all say the Bible verse. After you say the verse, you can start dancing again.

- Play "Movin' On" from the CD-ROM, and have the children dance around the room.
- Shine the flashlight. Have the children freeze in place.
- Help the child say the Bible verse. Play the game several times.

Live the Bible

Scroll Ornaments

Supplies: Leader Guide—p. 90, two six-inch lengths of ribbon or yarn for each child, ruler, crayons, hole punch

- Photocopy "Scroll Ornaments" once for every four children. Cut out one scroll for each child.

SAY: In Bible times, the Book of Isaiah was written on scrolls. Let's make a scroll ornament you can hang on your Christmas tree.

- Give each child a scroll. Read the Bible verse printed on the scroll.
- Let each child color both sides of the scroll with crayons.
- Show the children how to crumple their scroll picture and then smooth the picture out again. Encourage the children to crumple and smooth their scroll several times.
- Have the children spread their scroll out flat. Help each child roll the scroll into a small tube. Tie a length of yarn or ribbon around the tube.
- Punch a hole in one end of the scroll. Tie a loop of ribbon or yarn through the hole to make a hanger.

Night Lights

Supplies: glue, paper plates, clear jars or clear plastic cups, colored tissue paper, battery-powered tea lights

SAY: Let's make a night light to help us remember Isaiah's words.

- Pour glue onto the paper plates. Prepare one plate for every two children. Give each child a clear jar or cup.
- Let the children tear different colors of tissue paper into small pieces.
- Show the children how to dip the tissue paper pieces into the glue and then stick the pieces onto the jar or cup.
- Encourage the children to completely cover the outside of their jar or cup.
- Place a light inside each jar or cup. Turn on the light. Have each child hold his or her light, and say the Bible verse together.

Express Praise

Praise and Pray

Supplies: CD-ROM, CD player

- Sing with the children the song "Hear Us As We Pray" from the CD-ROM (lyrics on p. 86). Encourage the children to name any prayer requests.

PRAY: Thank you, God, for the prophets who told us about your plan for peace. Amen.

Blessing

Supplies: Bible Story Leaflets—Advent Take-Home, Songbook Take-Home; flashlight

- Have the children sit or stand in a circle.
- Shine the flashlight on one child. Avoid shining the light in the child's face.

SAY: *(Child's name)*, walk in the Lord's light.

- Continue until you have blessed each child.
- Send home "Advent Worship at Home" and "Bible Story Basics Songbook" with each child.

Isaiah

Let's walk by the L{ord}'s light. (Isaiah 2:5)

Mary's Story

Bible Verse: Let's walk by the Lord's light. (Isaiah 2:5)

Bible Story: Luke 1:26-38, 46-47

biblestorybasics.com

Bible Background

Our Bible story for this week is often called the Annunciation, referring to the time the angel Gabriel came to Mary with the news that she would have God's Son.

Mary was a young girl, probably 12 or 13 years old. This was the age at which girls were married during Bible times. She was engaged, or betrothed, to Joseph. In Mary's time, betrothal was a two-part action. In the first part, the woman legally became the property of the man. She could even be called his wife. The second part of betrothal took place about one year later, when there was actually a wedding ceremony and the wife went to live with her husband. Mary was in the first part of her betrothal to Joseph.

Mary was frightened by Gabriel's appearance and message. But the angel calmed her fears and told her that she would give birth to a baby boy named Jesus. The name *Jesus* is the Greek translation of the name *Joshua* (or, in Hebrew, *Yeshua*) and means "The Lord is salvation" or "God saves."

The angel continued with the news that Mary's baby would be God's Son and a great king. Mary still did not understand how this could happen. After all, she was only engaged, not married. But Gabriel reminded her that, with God, all things are possible.

Even though Mary might have been frightened or confused, her response was to answer God's call with a yes—"I am the Lord's servant. Let it be with me just as you have said" (Luke 1:38). This response is even more significant when we remember that Mary's pregnancy during her engagement would be considered a sign of adultery, and a woman caught in adultery could be stoned to death. Yet, Mary still responded to God's message with acceptance.

Devotion

As we draw closer to Christmas, we prepare once again to celebrate God's gift of love. Sometimes in the busyness of the season, it is possible to become overwhelmed. Take a moment to slow down and say a prayer of thanks to God for the message of love sent long ago and the many messages of love God continues to send us, sometimes in unexpected ways.

BASIC

Plan

Bible Beginnings
Welcome
Picture the Bible Story
Bible Puzzle
Bible Play

Into the Bible
Time for the Bible Story
Open the Bible
Experience the Bible Story
Say the Bible Verse

Bible Connections
Halo Hats
Angel Tag

Live the Bible
Angel Ornaments
Say Yes!

Express Praise
Praise and Pray
Blessing

Bible Beginnings

Welcome

Supplies: Class Pack—Attendance Chart, p. 4; CD-ROM; CD player; tape; offering basket

- Display the attendance chart (Class Pack) and "Unit 1 Bible Verse Picture" (Class Pack—p. 4) at the children's eye level.
- Play "The B-I-B-L-E" from the CD-ROM (lyrics on p. 85) as you welcome each child.
- Have each child mark his or her attendance.
- Show the children where to place their offerings on the worship table.

SAY: Today, our Bible story is about a young woman named Mary and an angel. The angel told Mary some surprising news.

- Point out the Bible verse picture, and say the Bible verse for the children.

Picture the Bible Story

Supplies: Leader Guide—p. 18, crayons or markers

- Photocopy "An Angel Visits Mary" for each child. Give each child the picture.
- Have the children fill in the missing lines and color the picture.

SAY: Today, our Bible story is about a young woman named Mary and an angel. The angel told Mary some surprising news. Mary was going to have a baby.

Bible Puzzle

Supplies: Bible Story Leaflets—Session 2, p. 4; crayons or markers

- Give each child a copy of today's Bible Story Leaflet.
- Encourage the children to circle five differences between the two angels pictured on the leaflet.

SAY: We see lots of angel ornaments at Christmas time. The ornaments remind us of the angel who visited Mary.

Bible Play

Supplies: plastic tub or box, crinkled or shredded paper, nonbreakable Nativity set

- Fill a plastic tub or box with crinkled or shredded paper.
- Hide the figures of Mary, Joseph, and an angel from the Nativity set in the paper.
- Encourage the children to dig through the paper to find the figures.
- Hide the figures again. Continue hiding and seeking the figures as time allows.

SAY: Today, our Bible story is about a young woman named Mary and an angel. The angel told Mary some surprising news. Mary was going to have a baby.

Into the Bible

Time for the Bible Story

SAY: Let's walk to our Story Area.

- Sing the following song to the tune of "Row, Row, Row Your Boat" as the children move. End the song in your Story Area.

SING: Let's walk by the light.
Let's walk by the light.
Joyfully, joyfully, joyfully, joyfully,
Let's walk by the light.

- Sing the song again, changing how the children move. (For example, sing, "Let's hop by the light," "Let's stomp by the light," or "Let's march by the light.") Continue singing and changing the suggested movement as time and interest allow.

- Have the children sit down.

SAY: These are the words of our Bible verse. Let's say it together: "Let's walk by the Lord's light" (Isaiah 2:5).

Open the Bible

Supplies: Bible Basics Storybook—pp. 190-191

- Tell the children the story "Mary's Story."

Experience the Bible Story

Supplies: CEB Bible; Bible Story Leaflets—Session 2, pp. 2-3

- Show the children the Bible.

TODAY'S BIBLE TOOL: Stories about Jesus are in the New Testament.

SAY: Our Bible has many stories. Some of the stories tell about the beginnings of God's people. These stories are in the Old Testament. Some of the stories tell about God's Son, Jesus. These stories are in the New Testament.

- Show the children the beginning of the New Testament. Then show the children the Book of Luke.

SAY: Today, our story is about something that happened to a young woman named Mary. It is in chapter one of the Book of Luke. Listen and watch as I tell the story. You can help me do some sounds and motions.

- Place the leaflet inside the Bible. Tell the children the story "Mary's Story" from the leaflet, and encourage them to say the words printed in bold and to do the suggested motions with you.

ASK: How do you think Mary felt when she heard the angel's news?

Say the Bible Verse

Supplies: Class Pack—p. 4, Leader Guide—p. 87

- Show the children the Bible verse picture (Class Pack). Repeat the verse.

- Teach the children signs in American Sign Language to go along with the verse (Leader Guide).
- Encourage the children to make the signs as they say the verse again.

Bible Connections

Halo Hats

Supplies: construction paper; scissors; tape; art supplies, such as glitter crayons, glitter markers, or gold or silver washi tape; gold or silver chenille stems; craft sticks

- Cut construction paper in half lengthwise. Tape the two lengths together to make one long strip. Prepare one strip for each child.
- Let each child decorate his or her strip with the art supplies.
- Give each child a chenille stem. Help each child make a circle out of the stem.
- Twist each child's circle around one end of a craft stick.
- Tape the craft stick on the decorated strip so that the child's halo sits over the inside of the strip.
- Wrap each child's strip around his or her head, and tape the ends of the strip together.
- Encourage the children to wear their halos.

SAY: In today's Bible story, an angel tells Mary that she will have baby Jesus.

ASK: How would you feel if you saw an angel?

Angel Tag

Supplies: tissue paper, chenille stem, jingle bell

- Twist a square of tissue paper, and thread a jingle bell onto a chenille stem. Then wrap the stem around the middle of the tissue paper to make angel wings.
- Have the children sit in a circle in an open area of the room.

SAY: An angel came to Mary to tell her the good news that she would have a baby.

- Choose one child to be the angel. Give the child the wings.
- Sing the following song to the tune of "A Tisket, a Tasket." Have the angel move around the outside of the circle. At the end of the song, the angel drops the wings behind one of the children sitting in the circle. That child jumps up and chases the angel around the circle until the angel reaches the empty spot. If the angel reaches the spot before the child can tag him or her, then that child becomes the new angel, picks up the wings, and continues the game.

SING: It's good news! It's good news!
    An angel came with good news!
    The angel said, "Don't be afraid;
    Just listen to my good news!"

Live the Bible

Angel Ornaments

Supplies: coffee filters, glitter crayons or glitter markers, wooden clothespins with spring, washable markers, ribbon or yarn, tape

SAY: At Christmas time, we see many kinds of angels. The angels remind us of the angel who brought Mary the good news about baby Jesus. Let's make an angel ornament to hang on your tree.

- Give each child a coffee filter. Have the child decorate the coffee filter with glitter crayons or glitter markers.
- Show each child how to scrunch the middle of the filter. Help the child clip the middle of the filter with a clothespin. This will make the angel's body and wings.
- Encourage each child to use a washable marker to add the angel's face at the end of the clothespin next to the wings. The child may also color the bottom of the clothespin to make the angel's clothes.
- Make loops of ribbon or yarn. Tape a loop onto the back of each clothespin to make a hanger.

Say Yes!

Supplies: none

SAY: Mary said she would do what God wanted her to do. Listen to me. If I say something you think God would want you to do, jump up and shout, "Yes!"

SAY: Love others. *(Shout, "Yes!")* Pray. *(Shout, "Yes!")* Take care of the earth. *(Shout, "Yes!")* Be mean to animals. *(Stay still.)* Share with my friends. *(Shout, "Yes!")* Help others. *(Shout, "Yes!")* Love God. *(Shout, "Yes!")*

Express Praise

Praise and Pray

Supplies: CD-ROM, CD player

- Sing with the children the song "Hear Us As We Pray" from the CD-ROM (lyrics on p. 86). Encourage the children to name any prayer requests.

PRAY: Thank you, God, for the good news about baby Jesus. Amen.

Blessing

Supplies: flashlight

- Have the children sit or stand in a circle.
- Shine the flashlight on one child. Avoid shining the light in the child's face.

SAY: *(Child's name)*, walk in the Lord's light.

- Continue until you have blessed each child.

An Angel Visits Mary

Let's walk by the Lord's light. (Isaiah 2:5)

Joseph's Story

Bible Verse: Let's walk by the Lord's light. (Isaiah 2:5)

Bible Story: Matthew 1:18-24

biblestorybasics.com

Bible Background

Of the four Gospels, only Matthew and Luke provide us with information about the birth of Jesus, and their accounts differ. Both Matthew and Luke tell of an angel delivering the news that Jesus would be born. In each case, the angel said the baby who would be born was to be named Jesus. However, as we heard last week, Luke tells us of an angel's visit to Mary. In Matthew, the story of the angel's visit concerns Joseph.

In the Bible, God often used dreams to send messages. This was the first of three visits an angel made to Joseph in a dream. In addition to the announcement of Jesus' upcoming birth, Joseph also received angelic instruction concerning taking Mary and Jesus to Egypt to escape Herod and returning to Israel after Herod dies.

Overall, the Bible mentions little about Joseph. We are told Joseph was a righteous man, and this statement is supported by his actions. Upon learning Mary was pregnant before they were married, Joseph made plans to divorce her quietly. In those days, once a couple was engaged, they were considered to be married. If Joseph had died during that time, Mary would have been considered a widow. For Mary to become pregnant before they had marital relations would have been considered adultery. Mosaic law required capital punishment under such cases. Even before the angel appeared to him, Joseph had already decided not to follow the law and have Mary stoned to death. After the angel's visit, Joseph took Mary as his wife.

Some people are hesitant to call Joseph the father of Jesus, since Jesus is God's Son. However, legally, Jesus was Joseph's adopted son. The Bible refers to Jesus as the son of Joseph and as the carpenter's son. It's through Joseph that Jesus' lineage is traced back to King David.

Devotion

Read Isaiah 7:14 and Matthew 1:23. *Emmanuel* is a Hebrew name meaning "God with us." The verse in Matthew refers back to the Old Testament Scripture in Isaiah. Matthew uses this passage to show his readers that Jesus fulfilled the Scriptures. "God with us" means that Jesus is truly divine ("God"), but also fully human ("with us"). Think back over the past week. How have you seen God with you?

BASIC

Plan

Bible Beginnings
Welcome
Picture the Bible Story
Bible Puzzle
Bible Play

Into the Bible
Time for the Bible Story
Open the Bible
Experience the Bible Story
Say the Bible Verse

Bible Connections
The Carpenter's Shop
Wake Up, Joseph!

Live the Bible
Jesus Name Ornaments
Name Game

Express Praise
Praise and Pray
Blessing

Bible Beginnings

Welcome

Supplies: Class Pack—Attendance Chart, p. 4; CD-ROM; CD player; tape; offering basket

- Display the attendance chart (Class Pack) and "Unit 1 Bible Verse Picture" (Class Pack—p. 4) at the children's eye level.
- Play "The B-I-B-L-E" from the CD-ROM (lyrics on p. 85) as you welcome each child.
- Have each child mark his or her attendance.
- Show the children where to place their offerings on the worship table.

SAY: Today, our Bible story is about a man named Joseph. Mary and Joseph were going to be married. One night, an angel visited Joseph in a dream. The angel told Joseph that Mary would have a baby named Jesus.

- Point out the Bible verse picture, and say the Bible verse for the children.

Picture the Bible Story

Supplies: Leader Guide—p. 24, crayons or markers

- Photocopy "The Angel and Joseph" for each child. Give each child the picture.

SAY: Today, our Bible story is about a man named Joseph and an angel. An angel came to Joseph in a dream and told Joseph some surprising news. Mary was going to have a baby.

- Encourage the children to decorate the picture with crayons or markers.

Bible Puzzle

Supplies: Bible Story Leaflets—Session 3, p. 4; crayons or markers

- Give each child a copy of today's Bible Story Leaflet.
- Encourage the children to connect the dots to complete the angel ornament.

SAY: Angel ornaments can help us remember the angel who spoke to Joseph in a dream.

Bible Play

Supplies: plastic tub or box, crinkled or shredded paper, nonbreakable Nativity set

- Fill a plastic tub or box with crinkled or shredded paper.
- Hide the figures of Joseph and an angel from the Nativity set in the paper.
- Encourage the children to dig through the paper to find the figures.
- Hide the figures again. Continue hiding and seeking the figures as time allows.

SAY: Today, our Bible story is about a man named Joseph and an angel. The angel told Joseph some surprising news. Mary was going to have a baby.

Into the Bible

Time for the Bible Story

SAY: Let's walk to our Story Area.

- Sing the following song to the tune of "Row, Row, Row Your Boat" as the children move. End the song in your Story Area.

SING: Let's walk by the light.
Let's walk by the light.
Joyfully, joyfully, joyfully, joyfully,
Let's walk by the light.

- Sing the song again, changing how the children move. (For example, sing, "Let's hop by the light," "Let's stomp by the light," or "Let's march by the light.") Continue singing and changing the suggested movement as time and interest allow.

- Have the children sit down.

SAY: These are the words of our Bible verse. Let's say it together: "Let's walk by the Lord's light" (Isaiah 2:5).

Open the Bible

Supplies: Bible Basics Storybook—pp. 136-137

- Tell the children the story "Joseph's Story."

Experience the Bible Story

Supplies: CEB Bible; Bible Story Leaflets—Session 3, pp. 2-3

- Show the children the Bible.

TODAY'S BIBLE TOOL: Stories about Jesus are in the New Testament.

SAY: Our Bible has many stories. Some of the stories tell about the beginnings of God's people. These stories are in the Old Testament. Some of the stories tell about God's Son, Jesus. These stories are in the New Testament.

- Show the children the Book of Matthew.

SAY: The very first book in the New Testament is the Book of Matthew. Our Bible story is from the first chapter in the Book of Matthew. Listen and watch as I tell the story.

- Place the leaflet in your Bible. Tell the children the story "Joseph's Story" from the leaflet.

ASK: How do you think Joseph felt when he woke up from the dream?

Say the Bible Verse

Supplies: Class Pack—p. 4, Leader Guide—p. 87

- Show the children the Bible verse picture (Class Pack). Repeat the verse.
- Teach the children signs in American Sign Language to go along with the verse (Leader Guide).
- Encourage the children to make the signs as they say the verse again.

Bible Connections

The Carpenter's Shop

Supplies: plastic table covering, wood scraps (without splinters), sandpaper of a variety of grits, markers, glue

- Cover the table with the covering.

SAY: Today, our Bible story is about a man named Joseph. Joseph was a carpenter. He made things out of wood.

- Place the wood scraps on the table. Let the children use the sandpaper to smooth the wood.
- Let the children color the wood with markers and glue pieces of wood together.

SAY: While Joseph was sleeping, God sent an angel to talk to Joseph in a dream. The angel told Joseph that Mary would have a baby named Jesus.

Wake Up, Joseph!

Supplies: none

SAY: One night, an angel came to Joseph in a dream. The angel told Joseph that Mary's baby would be God's Son. I want all of you to pretend to be Joseph. I will pretend to be the angel. Lie down on the floor, and pretend to sleep. If I tap you on the shoulder, then wake up and say the Bible verse.

- Practice the verse with the children: "Let's walk by the Lord's light" (Isaiah 2:5).
- Let the children pretend to sleep. Tap one child on the shoulder, and have the child wake up. Help the child say the Bible verse, if necessary.
- Continue the game until everyone has had a turn to say the verse.

Live the Bible

Jesus Name Ornaments

Supplies: plastic table covering, paint smocks, white construction paper, scissors, ruler, white crayon, tape, washable paints, paintbrushes, hole punch, yarn or ribbon

- Cover the table with the covering, and have the children wear paint smocks.
- Cut white construction paper into three-by-eight-inch strips. Each child will need one strip.

- Use a white crayon to write "Jesus" on each strip. Make heavy marks.
- Tape a strip on the table in front of each child.

SAY: Angels told both Mary and Joseph that Mary's baby would be named Jesus.

- Encourage the children to paint over the strip with washable paints. (The white crayon will resist the paint and show through.)
- Let the strips dry. Punch a hole in the top of each strip. Tie a loop of yarn or ribbon through the hole to make a hanger.

SAY: You can take your Jesus ornament home and hang it on your tree.

Name Game

Supplies: none

ASK: Who gave you your name?

SAY: Let's play a name game.

- Have the children sit in a circle.
- Say the name of a child in the circle. Clap with each syllable in the name.
- Repeat the name, and have all the children clap along with you.
- Continue around the circle, clapping with the syllables of each child's name.

SAY: The angel told both Mary and Joseph that Mary's baby would be named Jesus.

- End the game by saying and clapping with the name *Jesus*.

Express Praise

Praise and Pray

Supplies: CD-ROM, CD player

- Sing with the children the song "Hear Us As We Pray" from the CD-ROM (lyrics on p. 86). Encourage the children to name any prayer requests.

PRAY: Thank you, God, for the good news about baby Jesus. Amen.

Blessing

Supplies: Bible Story Leaflets—Christmas Send-Home, flashlight

- Have the children sit or stand in a circle.
- Shine the flashlight on one child. Avoid shining the light in the child's face.

SAY: *(Child's name)*, walk in the Lord's light.

- Continue until you have blessed each child.
- Mail "Christmas Storybook" to each child this week.

The Angel and Joseph

Let's walk by the L<small>ORD</small>'s light. (Isaiah 2:5)

Jesus' Story

Bible Verse: Let's walk by the Lord's light. (Isaiah 2:5)

Bible Story: Luke 2:1-7

biblestorybasics.com

Bible Background

Mary was pregnant when Caesar Augustus, the emperor of Rome, gave the order for a census. The purpose of the census was to raise tax money. Each man was required to go to the home of his ancestors. Because Joseph was part of the house of David, Mary and Joseph had to travel from Nazareth to Bethlehem.

There are two possible routes Mary and Joseph could have traveled from Nazareth to Bethlehem. The common belief is that they took the route that avoided Samaria, since Jews and Samaritans did not get along. This route would have taken them 20 or 30 miles out of their way into the Jordan Valley and through the Judean Desert. The second possible route was along the way known as the Road of the Patriarchs. This route was often used by pilgrims going to Jerusalem for Passover.

Travelers depended on the hospitality of townspeople. Strangers could expect to be welcomed in people's homes as they traveled; and for the time the travelers stayed, they were considered family. Because of the crowded conditions in Bethlehem, Mary and Joseph were unable to find a place to stay, either in a private home or in a guesthouse or inn. Some scholars suggest that the real reason Mary and Joseph were not given a room is that giving birth in the house would have made the house ritually unclean. Whatever the reason, God's Son was born in a space designed for animals.

When the time came for Mary to give birth, she did all the things a New Testament mother would have done. She washed her baby's body and rubbed him with salt. This custom was meant to firm and tighten the baby's skin. Then she wrapped him in bands of soft cloth. These bands kept the baby warm and helped his body grow straight and strong. Then Mary laid baby Jesus in a manger, a feeding trough for animals.

Devotion

December 25 is almost here. Are you ready? Or will you fill the next few days with shopping, baking, cleaning, wrapping, decorating, and on and on? Step out of all the busyness for a few minutes. How are you feeling? You're supposed to feel joyful, right? But holidays can be a time of joy or a time of sadness. Light a candle and think about the light God sends to each one of us through Jesus. When we walk by the Lord's light, we can have hope—even when we feel surrounded by the darkness.

BASIC

Plan

Bible Beginnings
Welcome
Picture the Bible Story
Bible Puzzle
Bible Play

Into the Bible
Time for the Bible Story
Open the Bible
Experience the Bible Story
Say the Bible Verse

Bible Connections
Swaddle the Baby
The Animals in the Stable

Live the Bible
Baby Jesus Ornament
Sing and Say

Express Praise
Praise and Pray
Blessing

Bible Beginnings

Welcome

Supplies: Class Pack—Attendance Chart, p. 4; CD-ROM; CD player; tape; offering basket

- Display the attendance chart (Class Pack) and "Unit 1 Bible Verse Picture" (Class Pack—p. 4) at the children's eye level.
- Play "The B-I-B-L-E" from the CD-ROM (lyrics on p. 85) as you welcome each child.
- Have each child mark his or her attendance.
- Show the children where to place their offerings on the worship table.

SAY: Today, our Bible story is about what happened when Jesus was born.

- Point out the Bible verse picture, and say the Bible verse for the children.

Picture the Bible Story

Supplies: Leader Guide—p. 30, crayons or markers

- Photocopy "Jesus Is Born" for each child. Give each child the picture.

SAY: Point to the donkey in this picture. Point to the cow. Now point to the sheep. Point to baby Jesus.

ASK: Where is baby Jesus sleeping? *(He's sleeping in a manger or feedbox.)*

SAY: Baby Jesus is sleeping in a manger or feedbox. It's a box where food is placed for animals to eat.

- Encourage the children to decorate the picture with crayons or markers.

Bible Puzzle

Supplies: Bible Story Leaflets—Session 4, p. 4; crayons or markers

- Give each child a copy of today's Bible Story Leaflet.
- Encourage the children to draw a line from baby Jesus to the things that could have been in the stable the night he was born.

SAY: The Bible tells us that baby Jesus was born in a stable. A stable is a warm, safe place where people can keep their animals, such as donkeys and cows.

Bible Play

Supplies: plastic tub or box, crinkled or shredded paper, nonbreakable Nativity set

- Fill a plastic tub or box with crinkled or shredded paper.
- Hide the figures of Mary, Joseph, baby Jesus, an angel, and any animals from the Nativity set in the paper.
- Encourage the children to dig through the paper to find the figures.
- Hide the figures again. Continue hiding and seeking the figures as time allows.

Into the Bible

Time for the Bible Story

SAY: Let's walk to our Story Area.

- Sing the following song to the tune of "Row, Row, Row Your Boat" as the children move. End the song in your Story Area.

SING: Let's walk by the light.
Let's walk by the light.
Joyfully, joyfully, joyfully, joyfully,
Let's walk by the light.

- Sing the song again, changing how the children move. (For example, sing, "Let's hop by the light," "Let's stomp by the light," or "Let's march by the light.") Continue singing and changing the suggested movement as time and interest allow.

- Have the children sit down.

SAY: These are the words of our Bible verse. Let's say it together: "Let's walk by the Lord's light" (Isaiah 2:5).

Open the Bible

Supplies: Bible Basics Storybook—pp. 192-193

- Tell the children the story "A Baby Is Born."

Experience the Bible Story

Supplies: CEB Bible; Bible Story Leaflets—Session 4, pp. 2-3

- Show the children the Bible.

TODAY'S BIBLE TOOL: Stories about Jesus are in the New Testament.

SAY: Our Bible has many stories. Some of the stories tell about the beginnings of God's people. These stories are in the Old Testament. Some of the stories tell about God's Son, Jesus. These stories are in the New Testament.

- Show the children the beginning of the New Testament. Then show the children the Book of Luke. Turn to the second chapter of Luke.

SAY: Today, our story is about what happened when Jesus was born. It is in chapter two in the Book of Luke. Listen and watch as I tell the story. You can help me do some sounds and motions.

- Place the leaflet inside the Bible. Tell the children the story "Jesus' Story" from the leaflet, and encourage them to do the suggested sounds and motions with you.

ASK: Where were you born? Were you born in a hospital? at home? in a stable like Jesus?

SAY: Close your eyes. Imagine being in the stable after baby Jesus was born.

ASK: What do you see in the stable? What do you hear?

Say the Bible Verse

Supplies: Class Pack—p. 4, Leader Guide—p. 87

- Show the children the Bible verse picture (Class Pack). Repeat the verse.
- Teach the children signs in American Sign Language to go along with the verse (Leader Guide).
- Encourage the children to make the signs as they say the verse again.

Bible Connections

Swaddle the Baby

Supplies: baby dolls, doll blankets or baby blankets

SAY: After Jesus was born, Mary wrapped him in cloth, like we wrap babies in blankets. This is called swaddling. Swaddling a baby makes the baby feel safe and warm.

- Explain how to swaddle a baby. Swaddle one of the dolls as you explain.
    1. Place the doll's back on the blanket, with its head on one corner of the blanket.
    2. Fold the corner on the opposite side of the blanket over the doll's body.
    3. Wrap one side corner around the doll's body. Wrap the other side corner around the doll's body. Tuck in the corners of the blanket.
- Let the children take turns swaddling the dolls.

The Animals in the Stable

Supplies: none

- Move to an open area of the room.

ASK: What animals do you think were at the stable when Jesus was born? *(Donkeys, cows, sheep, doves, goats, and chickens might have been in the stable.)*

- Say the following action poem, and encourage the children to move like each animal. You can also sing the poem to the tune of "The Farmer in the Dell."

The animals were in the stable.
The animals were in the stable.
On that special Christmas night,
The animals were in the stable.

The donkey walked like this.
(Walk like a donkey.)
The donkey walked like this.
On that special Christmas night,
The donkey walked like this.

The cow walked like this.
(Walk like a cow.)
The cow walked like this.
On that special Christmas night,
The cow walked like this.

The sheep walked like this.
(Walk like a sheep.)
The sheep walked like this.
On that special Christmas night,
The sheep walked like this.

The dove flew like this.
(Pretend to fly like a dove.)
The dove flew like this.
On that special Christmas night,
The dove flew like this.

Live the Bible

Baby Jesus Ornament

Supplies: wide craft sticks, scissors, tape, yarn, crayons or markers, tissues, glue

SAY: After baby Jesus was born, Mary wrapped Jesus in soft cloths. Let's make ornaments of baby Jesus wrapped in soft cloths.

- Use scissors to cut the wide craft sticks in half. Tape a loop of yarn to one side of each half. The side of the craft stick with the loop is now the back. Give each child half of a craft stick. Let the children use crayons or markers to make a face on the rounded end of the front of their craft stick.

- Show the children how to fold a tissue in half to make a triangle. Have each child make a tissue triangle. Have the children run a line of glue down the back of their craft stick, and then have the children place the glued side of the craft stick in the middle of their tissue triangle, with the stick's face above the fold of the tissue.

- Show each child how to wrap the tissue around the stick. Fold the bottom corner of the tissue over the stick, and then fold the side corners of the tissue around the stick. Have each child place a drop of glue on top of the folded tissue to secure it in place.

Sing and Say

Supplies: CD-ROM, CD player, baby doll wrapped in a blanket

- Have the children sit in a circle. Play "Joyful, Joyful" from the CD-ROM. Pass the doll around the circle, giving several children a turn to rock the baby.

- Stop the music. Have the child holding the doll say the Bible verse. Play the music again, and continue the game until each child has had a turn rocking the baby.

Express Praise

Praise and Pray

Supplies: CD-ROM, CD player

- Sing with the children the song "Hear Us As We Pray" from the CD-ROM (lyrics on p. 86). Encourage the children to name any prayer requests.

PRAY: Thank you, God, for baby Jesus. Amen.

Blessing

Supplies: flashlight

- Have the children sit or stand in a circle.

- Shine the flashlight on one child. Avoid shining the light in the child's face.

SAY: *(Child's name)*, walk in the Lord's light.

- Continue until you have blessed each child.

TIP: Save Christmas cards to use in next week's session.

Jesus Is Born

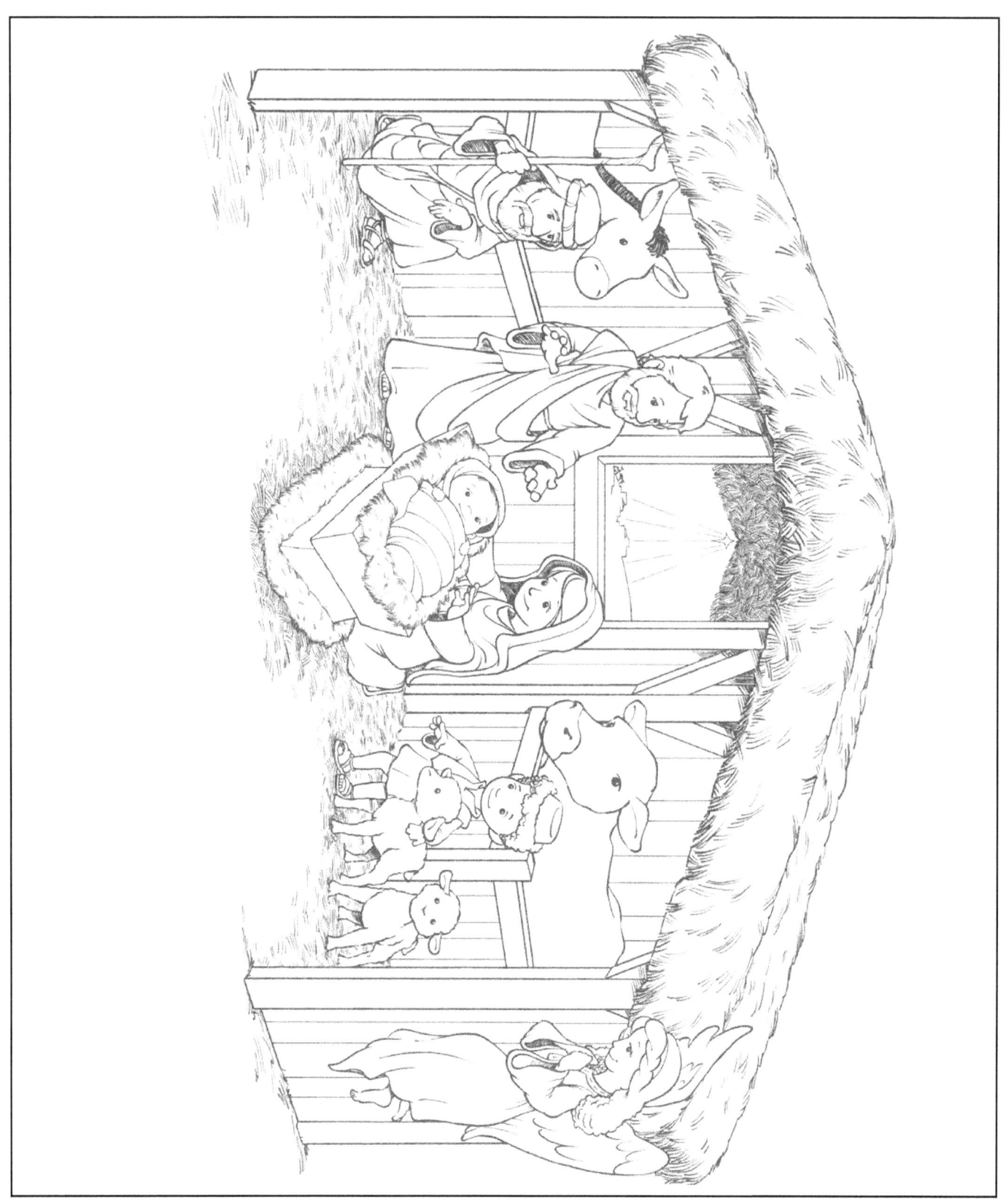

Let's walk by the Lord's light. (Isaiah 2:5)

Shepherds' Story

Bible Verse: Let's walk by the LORD's light. (Isaiah 2:5)

Bible Story: Luke 2:8-20

biblestorybasics.com

Bible Background

In Bible times, the life of a shepherd was hard. The fields around Bethlehem did not grow lush with grass. In order for their sheep to graze, shepherds moved the sheep around during the day. At night, the shepherds drove the sheep to a common place for protection. Sometimes the sheep were kept in a sheepfold. This was either an enclosure built with walls of rocks or a shelter built into a cave. One shepherd would lie down across the opening so that the sheep could not wander out during the night. Their work was often dirty, and they were considered unclean. This meant that they could not participate in many religious ceremonies, yet shepherds were the first to receive the news of Jesus' birth.

As with the angelic pronouncements to Mary and Joseph, the angel told the shepherds, "Don't be afraid!" Apparently, a message from God is nothing to fear. However, one can imagine that, to the shepherds who were used to being looked down upon, the sudden appearance of an angel and then a great assembly of angels must have caused some trembling. The angels, however, brought good news. In response to this surprising angelic announcement, the shepherds hurried off to Bethlehem. The shepherds' response is almost as surprising as the angels' visit. They didn't wait a couple weeks until they could arrange for someone to watch their sheep while they took a vacation. They didn't say, "That's interesting; next time we're in Bethlehem, we'll check it out." No, the shepherds "went quickly" to find Mary and Joseph and the child of whom they had been told (Luke 2:16). Once they had seen the baby, the shepherds went and told the good news to others.

Devotion

The shepherds outside Bethlehem were the first evangelists. When they heard the news, they hurried to see the newborn child. After they saw the baby, they told everyone they met the good news. You are an evangelist for the children you teach. Do your words and actions, like the words and actions of the shepherds, tell the good news?

When your children gather this week, they may have already celebrated Christmas with their families. For children, the celebration of Christmas is often equated with the presents they receive. Help them focus on celebrating the birth of Jesus.

BASIC

Plan

Bible Beginnings
- Welcome
- Picture the Bible Story
- Bible Puzzle
- Bible Play

Into the Bible
- Time for the Bible Story
- Open the Bible
- Experience the Bible Story
- Say the Bible Verse

Bible Connections
- Make Sheep Masks
- In the Stable

Live the Bible
- Make a Shepherd's Crook Ornament
- Christmas Cards

Express Praise
- Praise and Pray
- Blessing

Bible Beginnings

Welcome

Supplies: Class Pack—Attendance Chart, p. 4; CD-ROM; CD player; tape; offering basket

- Display the attendance chart (Class Pack) and "Unit 1 Bible Verse Picture" (Class Pack—p. 4) at the children's eye level.
- Play "The B-I-B-L-E" from the CD-ROM (lyrics on p. 85) as you welcome each child.
- Have each child mark his or her attendance.
- Show the children where to place their offerings on the worship table.

SAY: Today, our Bible story is about some shepherds. The shepherds were watching over their sheep when an angel suddenly appeared!

- Point out the Bible verse picture, and say the Bible verse for the children.

Picture the Bible Story

Supplies: Leader Guide—p. 36, crayons or markers

- Photocopy "Shepherds Hear Good News" for each child. Give each child the picture.

SAY: Today, our Bible story is about shepherds who were watching over their sheep. An angel suddenly appeared and told them the good news that Jesus was born.

- Encourage the children to decorate the picture with crayons or markers.

Bible Puzzle

Supplies: Bible Story Leaflets—Session 5, p. 4; crayons

- Give each child a copy of today's Bible Story Leaflet.
- Have each child use a finger or crayon to guide the shepherds to baby Jesus and then back home, making sure to pass by all the other people in the maze on the way.

SAY: The Bible tells us that, after the angel told the shepherds that baby Jesus was born, the shepherds hurried to see the baby. After they saw baby Jesus, they went back home, telling everyone they met about Jesus.

Bible Play

Supplies: plastic tub or box, crinkled or shredded paper, nonbreakable Nativity set

- Fill a plastic tub or box with crinkled or shredded paper.
- Hide the figures of Mary, Joseph, baby Jesus, an angel, any animals, and the shepherds from the Nativity set in the paper.
- Encourage the children to dig through the paper to find the figures.
- Hide the figures again. Continue hiding and seeking the figures as time allows.

SAY: After Jesus was born, shepherds came to the stable to see him.

Into the Bible

Time for the Bible Story

SAY: Let's walk to our Story Area.

- Sing the following song to the tune of "Row, Row, Row Your Boat" as the children move. End the song in your Story Area.

SING: Let's walk by the light.
　　　　Let's walk by the light.
　　　　Joyfully, joyfully, joyfully, joyfully,
　　　　Let's walk by the light.

- Sing the song again, changing how the children move. (For example, sing, "Let's hop by the light," "Let's stomp by the light," or "Let's march by the light.") Continue singing and changing the suggested movement as time and interest allow.

- Have the children sit down.

SAY: These are the words of our Bible verse. Let's say it together: "Let's walk by the Lord's light" (Isaiah 2:5).

Open the Bible

Supplies: Bible Basics Storybook—pp. 194-195

- Tell the children the story "The Shepherds Visit."

Experience the Bible Story

Supplies: CEB Bible; Bible Story Leaflets—Session 5, pp. 2-3

- Show the children the Bible.

TODAY'S BIBLE TOOL: Stories about Jesus are in the New Testament.

SAY: Our Bible has many stories. Some of the stories tell about the beginnings of God's people. These stories are in the Old Testament. Some of the stories tell about God's Son, Jesus. These stories are in the New Testament.

- Show the children the beginning of the New Testament. Then show the children the book of Luke. Turn to the second chapter of Luke.

SAY: Today, our Bible story is about some shepherds who were out watching their sheep at night when baby Jesus was born. It is from chapter two in the Book of Luke. Listen and watch as I tell the story. You can help me do some sounds and motions.

- Place the leaflet inside the Bible. Tell the children the story "Shepherds' Story" from the leaflet, and encourage them to say the words printed in bold and to do the suggested motions with you.

ASK: How do you think the shepherds felt when they saw all the angels?

Say the Bible Verse

Supplies: Class Pack—p. 4, Leader Guide—p. 87

- Show the children the Bible verse picture (Class Pack). Repeat the verse.
- Teach the children signs in American Sign Language to go along with the verse (Leader Guide).
- Encourage the children to make the signs as they say the verse again.

Bible Connections

Make Sheep Masks

Supplies: paper plates, scissors, stapler, tape, cotton balls, glue

- Cut the circular center out of each paper plate. Each child will use the rim of a paper plate to make a sheep mask.
- Cut the center of each plate in half to make sheep ears for each child.

SAY: Today, our Bible story is about shepherds. Shepherds take care of sheep. Let's make sheep masks and pretend to be sheep.

- Give each child a plate rim. Help each child staple his or her paper ears to the rim. Place a piece of tape over the prongs of each staple.
- Have each child glue cotton balls on his or her rim and ears.
- Show the children how to hold the rim in front of their face, and encourage them to pretend to be sheep.

In the Stable

Supplies: sheep masks from "Make Sheep Masks," optional: blindfold or sleep mask

- Have the children sit in a circle on the floor. If you have a large group of children, you may want to have them sit in more than one circle.

SAY: An angel told the shepherds that baby Jesus had been born. When the shepherds heard the good news about baby Jesus, they hurried to Bethlehem and found the stable.

ASK: Do you think the shepherds took the sheep with them when they went to find baby Jesus? If you were one of the shepherds, what would you have done?

SAY: Let's pretend we're sheep in the stable with baby Jesus and the shepherds. I will choose one of you to be "It." "It" will sit in the center of the circle blindfolded *(or with his or her eyes closed)*. I will choose someone to be a sheep. The sheep will hold up the sheep mask and say, "Baa," and we'll see if "It" can guess who is making the sound.

- Have "It" sit in the center of the circle. Help "It" put on the blindfold, or have "It" close his or her eyes. Point to a child in the circle. Have that child hold up his or her sheep mask and say, "Baa." Give "It" three opportunities to guess who is making the sound. If "It" guesses correctly, have the sheep become the next "It." If "It" guesses incorrectly each time, choose another person to be the sheep and have the same "It" guess again.

Live the Bible

Make a Shepherd's Crook Ornament

Supplies: chenille stems, beads

SAY: Shepherds used hooks, or crooks, to catch sheep who tried to wander away. Let's make shepherd's crook ornaments to remind us of the shepherds' visit to see Jesus.

- Make a knot on one end of each chenille stem. Give each child a stem.
- Show the children how to thread a bead onto the chenille stem. Encourage the children to keep threading beads onto their stem until the beads are almost at the end of the stem.
- Make a knot on the other end of each stem.
- Show the children how to bend the beaded chenille stem into the shape of a hook.

Christmas Cards

Supplies: construction paper, markers, recycled Christmas cards, scissors, glue

SAY: The shepherds told everyone they met the good news about baby Jesus. Let's make cards to tell others that Jesus is born.

- Give each child a piece of construction paper. Help the child fold the paper in half.
- Have each child write "Jesus is born!" inside his or her card. Write the words for younger children.
- Let each child decorate the cover of his or her card by gluing pictures cut out from recycled Christmas cards onto the cover of his or her card.

Express Praise

Praise and Pray

Supplies: CD-ROM, CD player

- Sing with the children the song "Hear Us As We Pray" from the CD-ROM (lyrics on p. 86). Encourage the children to name any prayer requests.

PRAY: Thank you, God, for baby Jesus. Amen.

Blessing

Supplies: flashlight

- Have the children sit or stand in a circle.
- Shine the flashlight on one child. Avoid shining the light in the child's face.

SAY: *(Child's name)*, walk in the Lord's light.

- Continue until you have blessed each child.

Shepherds Hear Good News

Let's walk by the L{ORD}'s light. (Isaiah 2:5)

Follow the Star

Bible Verse: Come, follow me. (Matthew 4:19)

Bible Story: Matthew 2:1-12

biblestorybasics.com

Bible Background

Today's story is from the Gospel of Matthew. This story is different from the birth story in Luke. Matthew's story is set among kings, priests, and magi, rather than mangers and shepherds.

The magi were Gentiles, traveling from the east. The Greek translation of *magi* means "wise men" or "astrologers." They were not kings. They were part of a priestly class of Persians or Babylonians who studied the stars and interpreted dreams. They were non-Jews who came searching for Jesus. They had not been waiting for the birth of the Messiah for hundreds of years, as the Jews had been. Rather, they came because they were astrologers who had seen a new star. They believed the appearance of a new star meant a king had been born, and they were curious. They were searching for this new king.

The magi's search led them to the current leader of Bethlehem, King Herod. King Herod's chief priests and scribes told Herod of Micah's prophecy that a new leader would be born in Bethlehem, and Herod told the magi to go to Bethlehem. They continued on their journey, following the star that led them to Jesus.

When they discovered Jesus, they worshipped him and offered gifts of gold, frankincense, and myrrh. The later tradition that there were three wise men comes from the three gifts. The Scriptures don't tell us how many magi made the journey.

Over the centuries, people have developed theories about these gifts and why the magi gave them to Jesus. Gold was an appropriate gift for royalty, and Jesus was the King of the Jews. Frankincense is an incense that was used in temple sacrifices. It referred to Jesus' sacrifice. Myrrh is an ointment that was used in preparing bodies for burial. This gift foreshadowed Jesus' burial.

Devotion

Read Mathew 2:1-12. Spend time reflecting on the magi. Their story conveys the message that God chose to send Jesus for everyone, even those who had not been waiting for his arrival and weren't fully aware of whom they were seeking. Like the magi, we receive the news of Jesus' birth with joy and honor him with gifts. Although we cannot bring gifts to Jesus in person, as the magi did, we can still honor Jesus with gifts of love and service.

BASIC

Plan

Bible Beginnings
Welcome
Picture the Bible Story
Bible Puzzle
Bible Play

Into the Bible
Time for the Bible Story
Open the Bible
Experience the Bible Story
Say the Bible Verse

Bible Connections
Star Poles
Star Parade

Live the Bible
Spices and Oils
Clay Stars

Express Praise
Praise and Pray
Blessing

Bible Beginnings

Welcome

Supplies: Class Pack—Attendance Chart, p. 5; CD-ROM; CD player; tape; offering basket

- Display the attendance chart (Class Pack) and "Unit 2 Bible Verse Picture" (Class Pack—p. 5) at the children's eye level.
- Play "The B-I-B-L-E" from the CD-ROM (lyrics on p. 85) as you welcome each child.
- Have each child mark his or her attendance.
- Show the children where to place their offerings on the worship table.

SAY: Today, our Bible story is about some magi. Sometimes we call magi "wise men." The magi saw a special star in the sky. The star led the magi to a new king.

ASK: Who do you think the new king was?

- Point out the Bible verse picture, and say the Bible verse for the children.

Picture the Bible Story

Supplies: Leader Guide—p. 42, crayons or markers

- Photocopy "Magi Bring Gifts" for each child. Give each child the picture.

SAY: The magi saw a special star in the sky. The star led the magi to a new king. Find the biggest star in the picture. The magi brought gifts of gold, frankincense, and myrrh to give to the new king. Find the gifts in the picture.

- Encourage the children to decorate the picture with crayons or markers.

Bible Puzzle

Supplies: Bible Story Leaflets—Session 6, p. 4; crayons or markers

- Give each child a copy of today's Bible Story Leaflet.
- Encourage the children to finish drawing each star in the picture. Let the children decorate the stars with crayons or markers, and then have the children circle the biggest star.

SAY: The Bible tells us that the magi followed a very bright star to find a new king.

Bible Play

Supplies: plastic tub or box, crinkled or shredded paper, nonbreakable Nativity set

- Fill a plastic tub or box with crinkled or shredded paper.
- Hide the figures of Mary, Joseph, baby Jesus, an angel, any animals, the shepherds, and the magi from the Nativity set in the paper.
- Encourage the children to dig through the paper to find the figures.
- Hide the figures again. Continue hiding and seeking the figures as time allows.

SAY: After Jesus was born, magi followed a bright star to find the young child.

Into the Bible

Time for the Bible Story

- Have the children line up behind you. Sing the following song to the tune of "London Bridge," and have the children walk behind you. Change how you move (tiptoe, hop, take giant steps, and so forth) as you lead the children to your Story Area.

SING: Jesus said, "Come, follow me.
Follow me. Follow me."
Jesus said, "Come, follow me.
Come and follow."

- Have the children sit down.

SAY: We just sang our new Bible verse. Let's say it together: "Come, follow me" (Matthew 4:19).

Open the Bible

Supplies: Bible Basics Storybook—pp. 138-139

- Tell the children the story "Follow the Star."

Experience the Bible Story

Supplies: CEB Bible; Bible Story Leaflets—Session 6, pp. 2-3

- Show the children the Bible.

TODAY'S BIBLE TOOL: Stories about Jesus are in the New Testament.

SAY: Our Bible has many stories. Some of the stories tell about the beginnings of God's people. These stories are in the Old Testament. Some of the stories tell about God's Son, Jesus. These stories are in the New Testament.

- Show the children the Book of Matthew. Turn to the second chapter of Matthew.

SAY: The very first book in the New Testament is the Book of Matthew. Our Bible story is from the second chapter in the Book of Matthew. Listen and watch as I tell the story. Every time I say the word *star* or *stars*, make the sign for *star* in American Sign Language.

- Teach the children the sign for *star*. Place the leaflet inside the Bible. Tell the children the story "Follow the Star" from the leaflet, and encourage them to make the sign for *star* with you.

ASK: How do you think the magi felt when they saw Jesus?

Say the Bible Verse

Supplies: Class Pack—p. 5, Leader Guide—p. 88

- Show the children the Bible verse picture (Class Pack). Repeat the verse.
- Teach the children signs in American Sign Language to go along with the verse (Leader Guide).
- Encourage the children to make the signs as they say the verse again.

Bible Connections

Star Poles

Supplies: Leader Guide—p. 91, scissors, curly ribbon or crepe paper streamers, small paper plates, glitter crayons, glue, star stickers, tape, large craft sticks

- Photocopy "Star Poles" for each child. Cut out the star circle from each copy.
- Cut curly ribbon or crepe paper streamers into 12-inch lengths. Each child will need several lengths.

SAY: The magi followed a bright star to find Jesus. Let's make star poles to help us remember the magi's journey.

- Give each child a small paper plate. Encourage each child to use glitter crayons to decorate around the edge of his or her paper plate.
- Give each child a star circle. Have each child glue his or her star circle onto the center of his or her plate.
- Let the children add star stickers all over their star circle.
- Tape a large craft stick to the back of each paper plate.

Star Parade

Supplies: star poles from "Star Poles," optional: magi costumes

- If you have magi costumes available, let the children dress up as magi.
- Have the children hold their star poles and line up behind you.

SAY: The magi followed the bright star to find Jesus. They had to travel a long time. Let's pretend we're the magi following the star.

- Lead the children on a journey around the classroom, the Sunday school hallways, or the entire church. End your journey back in your classroom.
- Sing the following song to the tune of "Twinkle, Twinkle, Little Star" as you walk.

SING: Twinkle, twinkle, shining star,
We are magi from afar,
Following a star so bright,
Looking for a king this night.
Twinkle, twinkle, shining star,
We are magi from afar.

SAY: When the magi found Jesus, they gave him gifts of gold, spices, and oils.

Live the Bible

Spices and Oils

Supplies: cotton balls, small paper cups, perfumes or scented oils, potpourri

- Place a cotton ball in a small paper cup. Pour a small amount of perfume or scented oil on the cotton ball. Prepare a cup for each perfume or scented oil.

- Place a small amount of potpourri in another cup.
- Have the children close their eyes. Hold the paper cups near their faces and encourage them to smell each cup.

ASK: What do you smell?

SAY: The magi brought gifts of frankincense and myrrh to Jesus. Frankincense and myrrh were spices and oils.

ASK: How do you think frankincense and myrrh smelled? Do you think these were good gifts for a young child? What would you have given Jesus? What are some things we can give to honor Jesus today?

Clay Stars

Supplies: measuring cup, flour, salt, water, large bowl, large spoon, star cookie cutters, unsharpened pencil, paper plates, marker, yarn or ribbon

- Let the children help you make self-hardening clay with the recipe below.

> Mix 4 cups of flour and 1½ cups of salt in a large bowl. Gradually add 1½ cups of water. Knead the dough with a large spoon until it sticks together.

SAY: The magi followed a star to find Jesus. Let's make clay stars you can give as gifts. When you give someone your gift, tell them the story of the magi.

- Give each child a portion of the dough. Let the children take turns using star cookie cutters to cut out a star from their portion of dough. Use an unsharpened pencil to punch a hole in each star. Place each star on a paper plate to dry. Write each child's name on the paper plate with his or her star.
- After the star dries, tie yarn or ribbon through the hole to make a hanger.

Express Praise

Praise and Pray

Supplies: CD-ROM, CD player

- Sing with the children the song "Hear Us As We Pray" from the CD-ROM (lyrics on p. 86). Encourage the children to name any prayer requests.

PRAY: Thank you, God, for the magi who followed the star to find Jesus. Amen.

Blessing

Supplies: small bowl of water, hand towel

- Go to a child. Dip a finger into the water, and then use your wet finger to draw a star on the back of the child's hand.
- Dry the child's hand with the towel.

SAY: *(Child's name)*, you are a follower of Jesus.

- Continue until you have blessed each child.

Magi Bring Gifts

Come, follow me. (Matthew 4:19)

Jesus Is Baptized

Bible Verse: Come, follow me. (Matthew 4:19)

Bible Story: Matthew 3:13-17

biblestorybasics.com

Bible Background

Matthew makes it sound like John came out of nowhere: "In those days John the Baptist appeared in the desert of Judea announcing, 'Change your hearts and lives! Here comes the kingdom of heaven!'" (Matthew 3:1). We know, however, from the account in Luke's Gospel that John was the child born to Zechariah and Elizabeth in their old age. Even before John's birth, Zechariah and Elizabeth were told John would be filled with the Holy Spirit and would turn many people to God. Luke also tells us Elizabeth was a relative of Mary, making John the Baptist and Jesus related. The Bible doesn't tell us whether John and Jesus knew each other as children. After Elizabeth gave birth to her son and she and Zechariah named him John, their neighbors wondered, "What then will this child be?" (Luke 1:66).

What became of this child? John grew up and went to live in the wilderness, wearing camel's hair, eating locusts and wild honey, baptizing people in the Jordan River, and exhorting people to acknowledge their sin and accept God's forgiveness. John encouraged people to be baptized as a way of preparing for the one who would come and bring the Holy Spirit to God's people.

And then one day, as John was going about the business of baptizing people, Jesus came from Nazareth to be baptized by John. As Jesus was coming out of the water, the heavens opened, the Spirit descended on him like a dove, and a voice from heaven claimed him as God's Son.

This lesson focuses on the biblical account of Jesus' baptism. You may want to use this as a springboard to talk about baptism in your own church.

Devotion

Read Matthew 3:17. Jesus heard these words as he came up out of the water of the Jordan River. Take a moment and hear God say these words to you. You are dearly loved by God. How does that make you feel? Do you claim these words with thanksgiving, or do you let negative self-talk tell you that you are unworthy of God's love? Henri Nouwen, in his book *Life of the Beloved: Spiritual Living in a Secular World*, says that, when we claim that we are beloved by God, it changes the way we live our everyday lives. Read Matthew 3:17 again, and this time hear God say, "This is my son, this is my daughter, whom I dearly love."

BASIC

Plan

Bible Beginnings
  Welcome
  Picture the Bible Story
  Bible Puzzle
  Bible Play

Into the Bible
  Time for the Bible Story
  Open the Bible
  Experience the Bible Story
  Say the Bible Verse

Bible Connections
  Handprint Doves
  Water Art

Live the Bible
  Happiness Jars
  Child of God

Express Praise
  Praise and Pray
  Blessing

Bible Beginnings

Welcome

Supplies: Class Pack—Attendance Chart, p. 5; CD-ROM; CD player; tape; offering basket

- Display the attendance chart (Class Pack) and "Unit 2 Bible Verse Picture" (Class Pack—p. 5) at the children's eye level.
- Play "The B-I-B-L-E" from the CD-ROM (lyrics on p. 85) as you welcome each child.
- Have each child mark his or her attendance.
- Show the children where to place their offerings on the worship table.

SAY: Jesus grew just like we grow. Today, our Bible story is from when Jesus was a man and was baptized in the water of a river by a man named John.

- Point out the Bible verse picture, and say the Bible verse for the children.

Picture the Bible Story

Supplies: Leader Guide—p. 48, watercolor paint, paintbrushes, cups of water

- Photocopy "John Baptizes Jesus" for each child. Give each child the picture.

SAY: This is a picture of Jesus and John. When John baptized Jesus, he dipped Jesus under the water and then lifted Jesus back up. When Jesus came up out of the water, a dove came down from the sky. The dove reminded Jesus that God loved him. Jesus knew that he was God's Son. Point to the dove in the picture.

- Encourage the children to decorate the picture with watercolor paint.

Bible Puzzle

Supplies: Bible Story Leaflets—Session 7, p. 4; crayons or markers

- Give each child a copy of today's Bible Story Leaflet.
- Encourage the children to connect the dots to make a dove. Let the children decorate the dove with crayons or markers.

SAY: After Jesus was baptized, a dove came down from the sky. The dove reminded Jesus that God loved him. Jesus knew that he was God's Son.

Bible Play

Supplies: water table or plastic tub, plastic cups, sieves, spoons, towels

- Partially fill a water table or plastic tub with water.
- Encourage the children to use the plastic cups, sieves, and spoons to play with the water.

TIP: Have towels ready to mop up spills and to dry the children's hands and arms.

SAY: Today, our Bible story is from when Jesus was a man and was baptized in a river by a man named John. When John baptized Jesus, he dipped Jesus under the water and then lifted Jesus back up.

Into the Bible

Time for the Bible Story

- Have the children line up behind you. Sing the following song to the tune of "London Bridge," and have the children walk behind you. Change how you move (tiptoe, hop, take giant steps, and so forth) as you lead the children to your Story Area.

SING: Jesus said, "Come, follow me.
Follow me. Follow me."
Jesus said, "Come, follow me.
Come and follow."

- Have the children sit down.

SAY: We just sang our Bible verse. Let's say it together: "Come, follow me" (Matthew 4:19).

Open the Bible

Supplies: Bible Basics Storybook—pp. 140-141

- Tell the children the story "Jesus Is Baptized."

Experience the Bible Story

Supplies: CEB Bible; Bible Story Leaflets—Session 7, pp. 2-3

- Show the children the Bible.

TODAY'S BIBLE TOOL: Stories about Jesus are in the New Testament.

SAY: Our Bible has many stories. Some of the stories tell about the beginnings of God's people. These stories are in the Old Testament. Some of the stories tell about God's Son, Jesus. These stories are in the New Testament.

- Show the children the Book of Matthew. Turn to the third chapter of Matthew.

SAY: The very first book in the New Testament is the Book of Matthew. Our Bible story is from the third chapter in the Book of Matthew. Listen and watch as I tell the story. You can help me do some motions.

- Place the leaflet inside the Bible. Tell the children the story "Jesus Is Baptized" from the leaflet, and encourage them to do the suggested motions with you.

ASK: How do you think Jesus felt when he saw the dove? How do you think Jesus felt when he heard God's voice?

Say the Bible Verse

Supplies: Class Pack—p. 5, Leader Guide—p. 88

- Show the children the Bible verse picture (Class Pack). Repeat the verse.

- Teach the children signs in American Sign Language to go along with the verse (Leader Guide).

- Encourage the children to make the signs as they say the verse again.

Bible Connections

Handprint Doves

Supplies: white and blue construction paper, crayons, safety scissors, glue, cotton balls, optional: white feathers

- Have each child place a hand onto white construction paper, with his or her fingers together and his or her thumb sticking out to the side. Trace each child's hand with a crayon. Help the child cut out the handprint. Let older children cut out the handprint themselves using safety scissors.
- Encourage the children to create a dove by drawing eyes and a beak on the thumb of their handprint.
- If you've provided white feathers, let the children glue the feathers onto their dove.
- Have each child glue his or her dove onto a piece of blue construction paper. Let the children glue cotton balls on the blue construction paper to represent clouds.

SAY: After Jesus was baptized, Jesus saw a dove flying down from the sky. He heard a voice say, "This is my Son whom I dearly love."

Water Art

Supplies: plastic table covering, spray bottle, construction paper, permanent marker, small pieces of tissue paper in a variety of bright colors

- Cover the table with the covering.
- Fill a spray bottle with water. Make sure the bottle sprays.

SAY: John baptized Jesus in the water of a river. Let's make a picture using water.

- Give each child a piece of construction paper. Encourage each child to place different pieces of tissue paper on his or her paper.
- Spray each piece of construction paper with the spray bottle.
- Remove the tissue paper from each page. See how the colors have bled onto the paper.
- Set the papers aside to dry.

TIP: Some brands of tissue paper don't bleed well. The cheaper brands usually work best. You can also order bleeding art tissue online.

Live the Bible

Happiness Jars

Supplies: Leader Guide—p. 92; scissors; plastic jars, other plastic containers, or resealable plastic bags; smiley face stickers

- Photocopy "Happiness Jar" for each child. Cut out each strip.
- Give each child a plastic jar, another kind of plastic container, or a resealable plastic bag.

SAY: When Jesus was baptized, he saw a dove flying down from the sky and heard God's voice say, "This is my Son whom I dearly love; I find happiness in him."

ASK: How do you think Jesus felt when he heard God's voice?

SAY: It makes us feel good when people say nice things to us. Let's each make a happiness jar that will help everyone in our families feel good.

- Let each child decorate the outside of his or her container with smiley face stickers.
- Read the strips to the children.
- Give each child a set of strips. Let each child place the strips inside his or her container.

Child of God

Supplies: none

- Have the children stand in a circle.

SAY: After Jesus was baptized he heard God's voice say, "This is my Son whom I dearly love; I find happiness in him." We are all children of God and loved by God.

- Say the following action poem, and lead the children in doing the motions.

> Child of God, touch your nose.
> Child of God, touch your toes.
>
> Child of God, turn around.
> Child of God, sit right down.
>
> Child of God, clap one, two, three.
> Child of God, tap one knee.
>
> Child of God, stretch up high.
> Child of God, wave goodbye.

Express Praise

Praise and Pray

Supplies: CD-ROM, CD player

- Sing with the children the song "Hear Us As We Pray" from the CD-ROM (lyrics on p. 86). Encourage the children to name any prayer requests.

PRAY: Thank you, God, for loving us. Amen.

Blessing

Supplies: small bowl of water, hand towel

- Go to a child. Dip a finger into the water, and then use your wet finger to draw a star on the back of the child's hand.
- Dry the child's hand with the towel.

SAY: *(Child's name)*, you are a follower of Jesus.

- Continue until you have blessed each child.

John Baptizes Jesus

Come, follow me. (Matthew 4:19)

Jesus Calls the Fishermen

Bible Verse: Come, follow me. (Matthew 4:19)

Bible Story: Matthew 4:18-22

Bible Background

In today's Bible story, Jesus began to gather his disciples. Having disciples was not unusual. Many teachers had disciples who stayed with them for years, learning from them through discussion and conversation. Sometimes a teacher would make arrangements for a student to become a disciple, but more often students asked for the honor of studying under the teacher. Jesus gathered disciples in a different way. Not only did he do all of his own choosing and calling, but he also looked for people in uncommon places—mostly in their workplace.

One of the first two disciples called by Jesus was Simon, whose name Jesus changed to Peter. The name *Peter* means "rock," and Peter would be important in founding the church. Peter's brother, Andrew, was also called to be a disciple. Jesus' next choice was another set of brothers, James and John. Some Bible scholars think that, because James and John are identified in the Gospels as the sons of Zebedee, their father may have been an important member of the early church. Peter, James, and John are mentioned at almost every important juncture in Jesus' history from this point on.

Matthew does not say why these fishermen dropped everything and followed without question. Some Bible scholars believe that these men had been acquainted with Jesus prior to Jesus calling them. They were not saying yes to a stranger. It's important that young children understand that Jesus called his friends to be his disciples. Do not let your children get the impression that it is okay to follow strangers because the disciples followed Jesus.

Talk with your children about being followers of Jesus. Children can understand that being kind to others and acting in loving ways, just as Jesus was kind and loving, are good ways to be followers of Jesus today.

Devotion

Remember how you received the call to teach. Was it from a pastor, children's minister, or volunteer committee? Or was it a frantic call from the Sunday school coordinator? No matter who actually invited you to teach, God made the call. Read Isaiah 6:1-8; 1 Samuel 3:1-10; and Matthew 4:18-22. God called Isaiah, Samuel, and the fishermen to tell others about God's love. Now you have the opportunity to tell the children you teach about God's love. Thank you for answering the call.

biblestorybasics.com

BASIC

Plan

Bible Beginnings
Welcome
Picture the Bible Story
Bible Puzzle
Bible Play

Into the Bible
Time for the Bible Story
Open the Bible
Experience the Bible Story
Say the Bible Verse

Bible Connections
Paper Plate Fish
Fishnet Tag

Live the Bible
J-E-S-U-S
Invite a Friend to Church

Express Praise
Praise and Pray
Blessing

Bible Beginnings

Welcome

Supplies: Class Pack—Attendance Chart, p. 5; CD-ROM; CD player; tape; offering basket

- Display the attendance chart (Class Pack) and "Unit 2 Bible Verse Picture" (Class Pack—p. 5) at the children's eye level.
- Play "The B-I-B-L-E" from the CD-ROM (lyrics on p. 85) as you welcome each child.
- Have each child mark his or her attendance.
- Show the children where to place their offerings on the worship table.

SAY: Today, our Bible story is about Jesus as a man. Jesus needed some helpers, so Jesus asked four fishermen to follow him. The four fishermen followed Jesus.

- Point out the Bible verse picture, and say the Bible verse for the children.

Picture the Bible Story

Supplies: Leader Guide—p. 54, crayons or markers

- Photocopy "Jesus Calls the Fishermen" for each child. Give each child the picture.

SAY: Jesus called four fishermen to follow him. This picture shows two of the fishermen. Their names were Peter and Andrew. They were brothers. When Jesus said, "Come, follow me," Peter and Andrew left their fishing nets to follow Jesus.

- Encourage the children to decorate the picture with crayons or markers.

Bible Puzzle

Supplies: Bible Story Leaflets—Session 8, p. 4; crayons or markers

- Give each child a copy of today's Bible Story Leaflet.

SAY: Jesus called four fishermen to follow him. The four fishermen were Peter, Andrew, James, and John. The four fishermen left their boats and nets and followed Jesus. They became Jesus' helpers.

- Encourage the children to circle the four footprints hidden in the picture.

Bible Play

Supplies: water table or plastic tub; plastic boats, foam trays, or sponges; towels

- Partially fill a water table or plastic tub with water.
- Encourage the children to pretend the boats, foam trays, or sponges are the boats of the four fishermen.

TIP: Have towels ready to mop up spills and to dry the children's hands and arms.

SAY: Today, our Bible story is about when Jesus called four fishermen to follow him.

Into the Bible

Time for the Bible Story

- Have the children line up behind you. Sing the following song to the tune of "London Bridge," and have the children walk behind you. Change how you move (tiptoe, hop, take giant steps, and so forth) as you lead the children to your Story Area.

SING: Jesus said, "Come, follow me.
　　　　Follow me. Follow me."
　　　　Jesus said, "Come, follow me.
　　　　Come and follow."

- Have the children sit down.

SAY: We just sang our Bible verse. Let's say it together: "Come, follow me" (Matthew 4:19).

Open the Bible

Supplies: Bible Basics Storybook—pp. 142-143

- Tell the children the story "Jesus Calls the Fishermen."

Experience the Bible Story

Supplies: CEB Bible; Bible Story Leaflets—Session 8, pp. 2-3

- Show the children the Bible.

TODAY'S BIBLE TOOL: Stories about Jesus are in the New Testament.

SAY: Our Bible has many stories. Some of the stories tell about the beginnings of God's people. These stories are in the Old Testament. Some of the stories tell about God's Son, Jesus. These stories are in the New Testament.

- Show the children the Book of Matthew. Turn to the fourth chapter of Matthew.

SAY: The very first book in the New Testament is the Book of Matthew. Our Bible story is from the fourth chapter in the Book of Matthew. Listen and watch as I tell the story. Each time I say, "Splash, splash, splash," I want you to repeat those words after me while rocking back and forth like we're in a fishing boat.

- Place the leaflet inside the Bible. Tell the children the story "Jesus Calls the Fishermen" from the leaflet, and encourage them to say the words printed in bold and to do the suggested motions with you.

ASK: How do you think the fishermen felt when Jesus asked them to be his helpers?

Say the Bible Verse

Supplies: Class Pack—p. 5, Leader Guide—p. 88

- Show the children the Bible verse picture (Class Pack). Repeat the verse.
- Teach the children signs in American Sign Language to go along with the verse (Leader Guide).
- Encourage the children to make the signs as they say the verse again.

Bible Connections

Paper Plate Fish

Supplies: paper plates, scissors, glue, crayons or markers, large sequins or circle stickers

- Cut a triangle out of one side of each paper plate.

SAY: Today, our Bible story is about what happened when Jesus asked four fishermen to be his helpers. Let's make fish to help us remember the story.

- Give each child his or her paper plate and triangle.

SAY: The area that has been cut off your plate is the mouth of the fish. The triangle will make the fish's tail.

- Have the children glue the triangle to the side of the plate opposite to the mouth.
- Let the children decorate the fish with crayons or markers.
- Encourage the children to add colorful scales to their fish by gluing on large sequins or sticking on circle stickers.

SAY: Jesus told the fishermen that they would fish for people instead of fish.

ASK: What do you think it means to fish for people?

Fishnet Tag

Supplies: none

- Have the children move to an open area of the room.

SAY: Jesus asked four fishermen to his helpers. Fishermen in Bible times fished with nets instead of fishing poles. Let's pretend we are fishermen in Bible times.

- Choose four children to be the net. Have these children hold hands to form a line. Have the remaining children be fish.

SAY: Let's pretend that these four children are the fishnet and the rest of you are fish. If you are caught by the fishnet, then you become part of the net.

- Let the fish "swim" around the room while the net tries to catch them. If a fish is tagged by the net, have the fish join the net. Let the children play until most of the fish are caught. Then choose four different children to be the net, and play again.

Live the Bible

J-E-S-U-S

Supplies: none

SAY: Let's sing a song that will help us learn to spell Jesus' name.

- Sing the following song to the tune of "B-I-N-G-O." Each time you repeat the verse, replace a letter of Jesus' name with a clap, until you are clapping in place of all five letters. (For example, on the first repetition, "J-E-S-U-S" will become "*(Clap.)*-E-S-U-S.")

SING: Jesus says to us, "Come, follow me."
Let's go and spell his name-o.
J-E-S-U-S
J-E-S-U-S
J-E-S-U-S
And Jesus is his name-o.

Invite a Friend to Church

Supplies: Leader Guide—p. 93, crayons or markers

- Write the name of your church on the line at the bottom of "Invite a Friend." Photocopy the invitation for each child. Give each child the invitation.

- Let the children decorate the invitation with crayons or markers.

SAY: One way we can follow Jesus is to invite friends to come to church with us.

Express Praise

Praise and Pray

Supplies: CD-ROM, CD player

- Sing with the children the song "Hear Us As We Pray" from the CD-ROM (lyrics on p. 86). Encourage the children to name any prayer requests.

PRAY: Thank you, God, for Jesus. Help us follow him. Amen.

Blessing

Supplies: small bowl of water, hand towel

- Go to a child. Dip a finger into the water, and then use your wet finger to draw a star on the back of the child's hand.

- Dry the child's hand with the towel.

SAY: *(Child's name)*, you are a follower of Jesus.

- Continue until you have blessed each child.

Jesus Calls the Fishermen

Come, follow me. (Matthew 4:19)

Beatitudes

Bible Verse: Come, follow me. (Matthew 4:19)

Bible Story: Matthew 5:1-12

Bible Background

Today's lesson takes a look at the Beatitudes. The Beatitudes are in similar, but not identical, forms in the Gospels of Matthew and Luke. In Matthew, the Beatitudes are the beginning of a series of Jesus' teachings known as the Sermon on the Mount. Matthew tells us that Jesus sat on the side of a mountain and taught a large group of his followers.

Although Matthew presents the Sermon on the Mount as one long sermon, it is more likely that Matthew gathers together into one place several teachings that Jesus shared at different times.

In the Beatitudes, we find instructions for how to live our lives. Jesus told us what we need to do to be "blessed" or "happy," depending on which translation you are reading. In this list of instructions, we find a description of how Jesus' followers should live. We also find reassurance that, when people treat us badly or when we grieve, God is with us to comfort and bless us.

The way Jesus taught us to live is sometimes different from how the world tells us to live. This was true for Jesus' followers who heard the Beatitudes originally, and it is true for us today. When Jesus prioritized the poor, the hungry, and those who grieve, he went against the accepted value system of the time. God calls us to depend on and obey God; to be humble, merciful, and pure of heart; and to be peacemakers, even when the world tries to get us to do otherwise. The reward for those who follow these teachings is great. They will receive God's comfort and deep joy and be rewarded in heaven.

Devotion

How are you feeling today? Are you tired? angry? sad? In the Beatitudes, Jesus teaches us that we can be happy—even when we're feeling other emotions too. We can be happy because God is with us, now and in the future. God is with us when we are grieving, and God will stay with us when the grieving is over, no matter when that might be. When Jesus preached on the mountain, he was talking to hurt, poor, and hopeless people, and his words didn't magically fix their problems. Instead, he showed them that, in spite of what they felt at that moment, remembering that God is with us, showing us the way to live, brings contentment.

biblestorybasics.com

BASIC

Plan

Bible Beginnings
Welcome
Picture the Bible Story
Bible Puzzle
Bible Play

Into the Bible
Time for the Bible Story
Open the Bible
Experience the Bible Story
Say the Bible Verse

Bible Connections
Happy Face Hats
Jesus Says

Live the Bible
Sing a Happy Song
Make a Happy Mural

Express Praise
Praise and Pray
Blessing

Bible Beginnings

Welcome

Supplies: Class Pack—Attendance Chart, p. 5; CD-ROM; CD player; tape; offering basket

- Display the attendance chart (Class Pack) and "Unit 2 Bible Verse Picture" (Class Pack—p. 5) at the children's eye level.
- Play "The B-I-B-L-E" from the CD-ROM (lyrics on p. 85) as you welcome each child.
- Have each child mark his or her attendance.
- Show the children where to place their offerings on the worship table.

SAY: Jesus taught many things about God. Today, our Bible story is about some teachings of Jesus called the Beatitudes. Jesus taught the Beatitudes to help us be happy and to help us learn what God wants us to do.

- Point out the Bible verse picture, and say the Bible verse for the children.

Picture the Bible Story

Supplies: Leader Guide—p. 60, crayons or markers

- Photocopy "Jesus Teaches" for each child. Give each child the picture.

SAY: Today, our Bible story is about a time when Jesus sat down on the side of a mountain. Many people came to see Jesus on the mountainside. Jesus taught the people about God. We call these teachings the Beatitudes.

- Encourage the children to decorate the picture with crayons or markers.

Bible Puzzle

Supplies: Bible Story Leaflets—Session 9, p. 4; crayons or markers

- Give each child a copy of today's Bible Story Leaflet.

SAY: Jesus went up on a mountain and taught people about God. We call these teachings from Jesus the Beatitudes. Jesus taught the Beatitudes to help us be happy and to help us learn what God wants us to do.

- Have the children circle the pictures that show children feeling happy and doing what God wants.

Bible Play

Supplies: play dough

SAY: Our Bible story is about some teachings of Jesus that are called the Beatitudes. *Beatitudes* is an important word to remember. It starts with the letter *b*.

- Encourage the children to make a B shape with the play dough.

SAY: Jesus taught the Beatitudes to help us be happy and to help us learn what God wants us to do.

- Encourage the children to make smiles and happy faces with the play dough.

Into the Bible

Time for the Bible Story

- Have the children line up behind you. Sing the following song to the tune of "London Bridge," and have the children walk behind you. Change how you move (tiptoe, hop, take giant steps, and so forth) as you lead the children to your Story Area.

SING: Jesus said, "Come, follow me.
Follow me. Follow me."
Jesus said, "Come, follow me.
Come and follow."

- Have the children sit down.

SAY: We just sang our Bible verse. Let's say it together: "Come, follow me" (Matthew 4:19).

Open the Bible

Supplies: Bible Basics Storybook—pp. 144-145

- Tell the children the story "Beatitudes."

Experience the Bible Story

Supplies: CEB Bible; Bible Story Leaflets—Session 9, pp. 2-3

- Show the children the Bible.

TODAY'S BIBLE TOOL: Stories about Jesus are in the New Testament.

SAY: Our Bible has many stories. Some of the stories tell about the beginnings of God's people. These stories are in the Old Testament. Some of the stories tell about God's Son, Jesus. These stories are in the New Testament.

- Show the children the Book of Matthew. Turn to the fifth chapter of Matthew.

SAY: The very first book in the New Testament is the Book of Matthew. Our Bible story is from the fifth chapter in the Book of Matthew. Listen and watch as I tell the story. Every time I say the word *happy*, make the sign for *happy* in American Sign Language.

- Teach the children the sign for *happy*. Place the leaflet inside the Bible. Tell the children the story "Beatitudes" from the leaflet, and encourage them to make the sign for *happy* with you.

SAY: Jesus taught the Beatitudes to help us be happy and to help us learn what God wants us to do.

ASK: When do you feel happy?

Say the Bible Verse

Supplies: Class Pack—p. 5, Leader Guide—p. 88

- Show the children the Bible verse picture (Class Pack). Repeat the verse.

- Teach the children signs in American Sign Language to go along with the verse (Leader Guide).
- Encourage the children to make the signs as they say the verse again.

Bible Connections

Happy Face Hats

Supplies: paper plates, scissors, crayons or markers

- Fold each paper plate in half. Cut around the circle in the middle of the paper plate, leaving about two inches of the circle still attached to the rim. Fold the circle up. The circle will become the happy face, and the rim of the plate will fit around the child's head, with the happy face sticking up. Prepare a paper plate for each child.

SAY: Jesus taught the Beatitudes to help us be happy and to help us learn what God wants us to do. Let's make happy face hats.

- Give each child a hat. Let each child use crayons or markers to make a happy face on the circle of his or her hat.
- Encourage each child to wear his or her hat.

Jesus Says

Supplies: none

SAY: With the Beatitudes, Jesus taught us that happy are people who trust God. Let's play a game called Jesus Says.

- Have the children move to an open area of the room. Stand in front of the children.

SAY: Listen carefully to what I say. If I begin by saying, "Jesus says," then do what I tell you to do. If I don't say, "Jesus says," stay still.

- Call out instructions, such as "Jesus says, 'Clap your hands'"; "Jesus says, 'Stand on one foot'"; and "Hop up and down."
- Keep all the children in the game for the whole game. If a child makes a mistake, say, "Oops, Jesus didn't say, 'Hop up and down.'" Then move on with the game.

Live the Bible

Sing a Happy Song

Supplies: none

SAY: The Beatitudes help us be happy and learn what God wants us to do.

ASK: What do you like to do when you're feeling really happy? Do you sing? Do you shout? Do you do a happy dance?

- Say the following action poem, and lead the children in doing the motions. You can also sing the poem to the tune of "Did You Ever See a Lassie?"

If you're feeling happy,
So happy, so happy,
If you're feeling happy,
Then turn all around.
(Turn around.)
Turning and turning,
And turning and turning.
If you're feeling happy,
Then turn all around.

If you're feeling happy,
So happy, so happy,
If you're feeling happy,
Then wiggle your hips.
(Wiggle your hips.)
Wiggle and wiggle,
And wiggle and wiggle.
If you're feeling happy,
Then wiggle your hips.

If you're feeling happy,
So happy, so happy,
If you're feeling happy,
Then shake out your foot.
(Shake out your foot.)
Shaking and shaking,
And shaking and shaking.
If you're feeling happy,
Then shake out your foot.

If you're feeling happy,
So happy, so happy,
If you're feeling happy,
Then jump up and down.
(Jump.)
Jumping and jumping,
And jumping and jumping.
If you're feeling happy,
Then jump up and down.

Make a Happy Mural

Supplies: permanent marker, mural paper, crayons or markers, stickers

- Use a permanent marker to write the word *happy* in big bubble letters across a large piece of mural paper.
- Let the children decorate the mural by using crayons or markers to color in the letters with happy colors.
- Encourage the children to add colorful stickers to the mural.

Express Praise

Praise and Pray

Supplies: CD-ROM, CD player

- Sing with the children the song "Hear Us As We Pray" from the CD-ROM (lyrics on p. 86). Encourage the children to name any prayer requests.

PRAY: Thank you, God, for Jesus. Help us pay attention to his teachings. Amen.

Blessing

Supplies: small bowl of water, hand towel

- Go to a child. Dip a finger into the water, and then use your wet finger to draw a star on the back of the child's hand.
- Dry the child's hand with the towel.

SAY: *(Child's name)*, you are a follower of Jesus.

- Continue until you have blessed each child.

Jesus Teaches

Come, follow me. (Matthew 4:19)

The Lord's Prayer

Bible Verse: Everybody who hears these words of mine and puts them into practice is like a wise builder. (Matthew 7:24)

Bible Story: Matthew 6:5-15

biblestorybasics.com

Bible Background

Jesus began his lesson on prayer by explaining how not to pray. Jesus warned against insincere and showy prayer (Matthew 6:5). In Jesus' time, it was common for people to pray in public in the synagogue. While Jesus was not teaching against public prayer, he was issuing a reminder that the focus of prayer should be God, not other people. Jesus also assured us that God already knows our prayers before we speak them. Here was an assurance for those who might worry about not knowing the right words to say.

Jesus begins his prayer by addressing God as "our Father who is in heaven" (6:9). This is a simple yet powerful phrase. The words *in heaven* remind us God reigns with heavenly authority, yet the use of the word *father* establishes our relationship with God as a close, personal one. As great and wonderful as God is, God loves us deeply and unconditionally, as an ideal parent does. The word *our* reminds those who pray this prayer that we are a community. Yes, we can pray those words individually, but they are words that link us together and remind us of the common bond we have as beloved children of God.

Compared to most prayers used in Jesus' time, the Lord's Prayer is short. Jesus drew on Jewish prayers when he prayed, but the example he offered was unique in it simplicity and brevity. Even in its simplicity, the Lord's Prayer encompasses important aspects of prayer. The prayer includes adoration, confession, thanksgiving, and supplication. We can pray the Lord's Prayer as we were taught it, and we can also use it as a model of prayer.

As you teach your children the Lord's Prayer, use the wording used in your church. This is a wonderful opportunity to familiarize children with words they will hear and say often in worship.

Devotion

Take time to pray the Lord's Prayer, knowing these words have been prayed by many others before you and will be prayed by many others after you. Pray it knowing you are loved by the one to whom we pray and the one who taught us to pray.

BASIC

Plan

Bible Beginnings
Welcome
Picture the Bible Story
Bible Puzzle
Bible Play

Into the Bible
Time for the Bible Story
Open the Bible
Experience the Bible Story
Say the Bible Verse

Bible Connections
Paint a Prayer
A Special Place to Pray

Live the Bible
Prayer Walk
Paper Bag Prayers

Express Praise
Praise and Pray
Blessing

Bible Beginnings

Welcome

Supplies: Class Pack—Attendance Chart, p. 6; CD-ROM; CD player; tape; offering basket

- Display the attendance chart (Class Pack) and "Unit 3 Bible Verse Picture" (Class Pack—p. 6) at the children's eye level.
- Play "The B-I-B-L-E" from the CD-ROM (lyrics on p. 85) as you welcome each child.
- Have each child mark his or her attendance.
- Show the children where to place their offerings on the worship table.

SAY: Today, our Bible story is about a special prayer Jesus taught the people to pray. We call this prayer the Lord's Prayer. Praying is talking to God.

- Point out the Bible verse picture, and say the Bible verse for the children.

Picture the Bible Story

Supplies: Leader Guide—p. 66, crayons or markers

- Photocopy "Jesus Teaches the Lord's Prayer" for each child. Give each child the picture.

SAY: Jesus taught the people a special prayer to help them talk to God. We call this prayer the Lord's Prayer.

- Encourage the children to decorate the picture with crayons or markers.

Bible Puzzle

Supplies: Bible Story Leaflets—Session 10, p. 4; crayons or markers

- Give each child a copy of today's Bible Story Leaflet.
- Encourage the children to connect the dots to make the praying hands.

SAY: Today, our Bible story is about a special prayer Jesus taught the people to pray. We call this prayer the Lord's Prayer. Sometimes people hold their hands like this when they pray.

Bible Play

Supplies: interlocking blocks or wood blocks

- Encourage the children to build houses with the blocks.

SAY: We have a new Bible verse today. The Bible verse is "Everybody who hears these words of mine and puts them into practice is like a wise builder" (Matthew 7:24).

ASK: How do your think a wise builder builds a house? Does the builder build with straw or sticks, like two of the three little pigs? Does the wise builder build with wood and brick?

SAY: Jesus wanted the people to pay attention to the things he was teaching. He wanted them to be wise.

Into the Bible

Time for the Bible Story

- Sing the following song to the tune of "Do You Know The Muffin Man?" as the children move. End the song in your Story Area.

SING: Do you know this special prayer,
Special prayer, special prayer?
Do you know this special prayer
That Jesus taught his friends?

- Have the children sit down.

SAY: Jesus taught his friends a special prayer to help them talk to God. We call this prayer the Lord's Prayer. We can find this prayer in the Bible.

Open the Bible

Supplies: Bible Basics Storybook—pp. 146-147

- Tell the children the story "The Lord's Prayer."

Experience the Bible Story

Supplies: CEB Bible; Bible Story Leaflets—Session 10, pp. 2-3

- Show the children the Bible.

TODAY'S BIBLE TOOL: The teachings of Jesus are in the New Testament.

SAY: Our Bible has many stories. Some of the stories tell about the beginnings of God's people. These stories are in the Old Testament. Some of the stories are about things that Jesus taught us. These stories are in the New Testament.

- Show the children the Book of Matthew. Turn to the sixth chapter of Matthew.

SAY: The very first book in the New Testament is the Book of Matthew. Our Bible story is from the sixth chapter in the Book of Matthew. Listen and watch as I tell the story. You can help me do some sounds and motions.

- Place the leaflet inside the Bible. Tell the children the story "The Lord's Prayer" from the leaflet, and encourage them to say the words printed in bold and to do the suggested motions with you.

SAY: Prayer is talking to God. Jesus taught us a special prayer called the Lord's Prayer.

ASK: When is a good time to pray?

Say the Bible Verse

Supplies: Class Pack—p. 6, Leader Guide—p. 89

- Show the children the Bible verse picture (Class Pack). Repeat the verse.
- Teach the children signs in American Sign Language to go along with the verse (Leader Guide).
- Encourage the children to make the signs as they say the verse again.

Bible Connections

Paint a Prayer

Supplies: Leader Guide—p. 94, plastic table covering, paint smocks, watercolor paint, paintbrushes

- Photocopy "The Lord's Prayer" for each child.
- Cover the table with the covering, and have the children wear the smocks.

SAY: Today, our Bible story is about a special prayer Jesus taught the people. We call this prayer the Lord's Prayer.

- Give each child a copy of "The Lord's Prayer." Set out the paint and paintbrushes for the children to share.

SAY: Listen as I pray this special prayer. While I am praying, I want you to paint over the prayer with the watercolor paints. The words of the prayer will show through the paint.

- Softly read the version of the Lord's Prayer on "The Lord's Prayer."

ASK: How do you feel when you hear the prayer?

A Special Place to Pray

Supplies: Class Pack, Bible Basics Storybook, small tent or sheet, pillows, stuffed animals, blanket, flashlight, books

SAY: Sometimes we all pray together, and sometimes we want to be alone when we pray. Let's make a special place to pray in our room.

- Have the children help you move a small table to a corner of the room and cover it with a sheet, or set up a small tent in a corner of the room.
- Have the children place pillows, a flashlight, a copy of the Bible Basics Storybook, and some of the Bible verse pictures from the Class Pack inside the special prayer place.

SAY: When you want to be quiet or to talk to God by yourself, you can crawl into our special place to pray. You can sit on the pillows and use the flashlight to look at the storybook and the Bible verse pictures.

- Encourage each child to spend a few minutes in the special prayer place.

Live the Bible

Prayer Walk

Supplies: none

- Have the children line up behind you.

SAY: Today, our Bible story is about a special prayer Jesus taught the people. Prayer is talking to God. We can pray to God anytime and anywhere. God hears us when we pray. Let's take a prayer walk.

- Lead the children on a walk through the church.
- Stop outside the nursery.

SAY: Thank you, God, for all the babies in our nursery. Amen.

- Continue walking around the church, stopping and saying prayers for different classes and different places in the church, such as the playground, sanctuary, and garden.
- If you need to stay in your classroom, take a walk around the room, stopping to say prayers thanking God for blocks, baby dolls, art supplies, tables, and so forth.

Paper Bag Prayers

Supplies: paper lunch bag; a small item to place inside the bag, such as an apple, an orange, a leaf, a flower, a small baby doll, a toy car, or a plastic animal

- Place the item inside the lunch bag.
- Have the children sit in a circle.
- Pass the bag around the circle. Have each child reach into the bag and feel the item. (No peeking!) When the bag has been around the circle, ask the children to guess what is in the bag.
- After they respond, pull the item out of the bag and show it to the children.
- Say a prayer, thanking God for the item or what the item represents. For instance, if the item is a baby doll, thank God for toys or babies.

SAY: Prayer is talking to God. One kind of prayer is a thank-you prayer. We can thank God for things that God has made, such as trees and flowers. We thank God for things that make us happy, such as toys and friends. We can thank God for anything!

Express Praise

Praise and Pray

Supplies: CD-ROM, CD player

- Sing with the children the song "Hear Us As We Pray" from the CD-ROM (lyrics on p. 86). Encourage the children to name any prayer requests.

PRAY: Thank you, God, for the special prayer Jesus taught us to pray. Amen.

Blessing

Supplies: child-safe mirror

- Hand one child the mirror. Have the child look into the mirror.

SAY: Thank you, God, for *(child's name)*.

- Continue passing the mirror until you have blessed each child.
- Say the Lord's Prayer together.

Jesus Teaches the Lord's Prayer

Everybody who hears these words of mine and puts them into practice is like a wise builder. (Matthew 7:24)

The Birds in the Sky

Bible Verse: Everybody who hears these words of mine and puts them into practice is like a wise builder. (Matthew 7:24)

Bible Story: Matthew 6:25-34

biblestorybasics.com

Bible Background

There are so many things in life we can worry about. Will we have enough money to pay our bills? What will happen if we get sick? Will our children grow up healthy, safe, and happy? The list of worries can become endless once we begin to name these things.

In Matthew 6:25, we read that Jesus said, "Don't worry about your life, what you'll eat or what you'll drink, or about your body, what you'll wear." Jesus went on to say that just as God provides for the birds and the flowers, God will also provide for us. These words can be comforting, but they are more than that. There is a reason we are not to worry, and that reason is revealed in Matthew 6:33, when Jesus said, "Desire first and foremost God's kingdom and God's righteousness." We are not to worry, because it distracts us from what is important. We are to put God first, not our concerns about physical needs. This is a passage about getting our priorities straight.

Does this mean we no longer need to work or be responsible with our money? If God will provide for us, can we simply relax and do nothing? No. Although God is capable of providing manna from heaven, as God did for the Israelites, the means of God's provision is more often through the efforts of those that love God. We are the hearts and hands of God. We must work and plan to take care of ourselves and our families, but we must first and foremost trust in God. By focusing on God and spending time discovering what God wants us to do and to be, we may just find that we don't have time to worry.

Adults are not the only ones capable of worrying. Although the focus of worry may be different for adults, children are capable of finding plenty to worry about. Help your children know that, no matter what worries they are facing, they can trust in God. Remind them that God is always with us and taking care of us.

Devotion

It's easy to get caught up in our worries, but this Scripture reminds us to trust God and to put God first. But how do we do put aside our worries and trust God? We can start with prayer and with reading the Bible. Here are some Scriptures to get you started: Psalm 23:1-6; Psalm 46:1-3; Isaiah 41:10; Mark 5:36; and Romans 8:38-39.

BASIC

Plan

Bible Beginnings
- Welcome
- Picture the Bible Story
- Bible Puzzle
- Bible Play

Into the Bible
- Time for the Bible Story
- Open the Bible
- Experience the Bible Story
- Say the Bible Verse

Bible Connections
- Make Flowers
- Bird Race

Live the Bible
- Jesus Taught
- Bubble Prayers

Express Praise
- Praise and Pray
- Blessing

Bible Beginnings

Welcome

Supplies: Class Pack—Attendance Chart, p. 6; CD-ROM; CD player; tape; offering basket

- Display the attendance chart (Class Pack) and "Unit 3 Bible Verse Picture" (Class Pack—p. 6) at the children's eye level.
- Play "The B-I-B-L-E" from the CD-ROM (lyrics on p. 85) as you welcome each child.
- Have each child mark his or her attendance.
- Show the children where to place their offerings on the worship table.

SAY: Today, our Bible story is something Jesus told the people who came to hear him teach about God. Jesus said that God cares about the birds and flowers—and that God cares about us.

- Point out the Bible verse picture, and say the Bible verse for the children.

Picture the Bible Story

Supplies: Leader Guide—p. 72, crayons or markers

- Photocopy "Look at the Birds" for each child. Give each child the picture.

SAY: Jesus said that God cares about the birds and flowers—and that God cares about us.

- Encourage the children to decorate the picture with crayons or markers.

Bible Puzzle

Supplies: Bible Story Leaflets—Session 11, p. 4; crayons or markers

- Give each child a copy of today's Bible Story Leaflet.
- Encourage the children to draw a line from the bird or flower in the column on the left to the matching bird or flower in the column on the right.

SAY: Jesus taught the people that God cares about the birds and flowers—and that God cares about us.

Bible Play

Supplies: interlocking blocks or wood blocks

- Encourage the children to build houses with the blocks.

SAY: Our Bible verse is "Everybody who hears these words of mine and puts them into practice is like a wise builder" (Matthew 7:24).

ASK: How do your think a wise builder builds a house? Does the builder build with straw or sticks, like two of the three little pigs? Does the wise builder build with wood and brick?

SAY: Jesus wanted the people to pay attention to the things he was teaching. He wanted the people to be wise.

Into the Bible

Time for the Bible Story

- Sing the following song to the tune of "Do You Know The Muffin Man?" as the children move. End the song in your Story Area.

SING: Do you know this special prayer,
Special prayer, special prayer?
Do you know this special prayer
That Jesus taught his friends?

- Have the children sit down.

SAY: Jesus taught the people the Lord's Prayer and that God cares about the birds and flowers—and that God cares about us.

Open the Bible

Supplies: Bible Basics Storybook—pp. 148-149

- Tell the children the story "The Birds in the Sky."

Experience the Bible Story

Supplies: CEB Bible; Bible Story Leaflets—Session 11, pp. 2-3

- Show the children the Bible.

TODAY'S BIBLE TOOL: The teachings of Jesus are in the New Testament.

SAY: Our Bible has many stories. Some of the stories tell about the beginnings of God's people. These stories are in the Old Testament. Some of the stories are about things that Jesus taught us. These stories are in the New Testament.

- Show the children the Book of Matthew. Turn to the sixth chapter of Matthew.

SAY: The very first book in the New Testament is the Book of Matthew. Our Bible story is from the sixth chapter in the Book of Matthew. Listen and watch as I tell the story. You can help me do some sounds and motions.

- Place the leaflet inside the Bible. Tell the children the story "The Birds in the Sky" from the leaflet, and encourage them to say the words printed in bold and to do the suggested motions with you.

SAY: Jesus taught the people that God cares about the birds and flowers—and that God cares about us.

Say the Bible Verse

Supplies: Class Pack—p. 6, Leader Guide—p. 89

- Show the children the Bible verse picture (Class Pack). Repeat the verse.
- Teach the children signs in American Sign Language to go along with the verse (Leader Guide).
- Encourage the children to make the signs as they say the verse again.

Bible Connections

Make Flowers

Supplies: colorful baking paper in small, medium, and large sizes; glue; buttons or circle stickers; craft sticks

- Give each child a piece of baking paper in each of the three sizes.
- Show the children how to make a flower by gluing the medium-sized paper in the center of the large-sized paper and then gluing the small-sized paper in the center of the medium-sized paper.
- Let each child add a center to his or her flower by gluing a button or sticking a circle sticker on the center of the small-sized paper.
- Glue a craft stick on the back of each flower.

ASK: What is your favorite flower?

SAY: You all made beautiful flowers. Jesus taught the people that God cares about the flowers—and that God cares about us.

Bird Race

Supplies: medium-sized ball, masking tape

- Move to an open area of the room.
- Use masking tape to mark a starting line and a finish line on the floor.
- Have the children line up behind the starting line.

TIP: If you have a large group of children, divide them into two or more groups.

SAY: Birds are important in today's Bible story. There are many different kinds of birds, and they move in different ways. Let's pretend to be different kinds of birds. First, let's pretend to be chickens. Put your hands on your hips. Your elbows will be your wings. Flap your wings, and walk like a chicken toward the finish line. You might stop along the way and peck at the ground for food.

- Have the children walk across the room like chickens.

SAY: Another kind of bird is the flamingo. Flamingos are pink. They like to stand on one leg. Let me see you stand on one leg.

- Have the children stand on one leg.

SAY: Another kind of bird is the penguin. Most penguins are black and white. They waddle when they walk. One of us is going to waddle like a penguin.

- Give the ball to a child. Have the child place the ball between his or her knees. Then have the child walk back to the starting line with the ball between his or her knees.

SAY: Most birds can fly. Let's fly back to the starting line.

- Have the rest of the children pretend to fly back to the starting line.

SAY: Jesus taught the people that God cares about the birds—and that God cares about us.

Live the Bible

Jesus Taught

Supplies: none

SAY: Jesus taught the people that God cares about the birds and flowers—and that God cares about us.

- Say the following action poem, and lead the children in doing the motions. Repeat the poem several times, changing "Clap your hands!" to "Stomp your feet!" and then "Turn around!" You can also sing the poem to the tune of "London Bridge."

    Jesus taught God cares for us. *(Fold your hands over your heart.)*
    Clap your hands! Shout, "Hurray!" *(Clap your hands; jab your hand into the air.)*
    Jesus taught God cares for us. *(Fold your hands over your heart.)*
    Thank you, God.

Bubble Prayers

Supplies: bubble solution, bubble wands

SAY: Jesus wanted the people to know that we don't have to worry because we can trust God to take care of us.

ASK: What is something you're worrying about today?

SAY: We can talk to God about our worries. Let's use bubbles to talk to God right now.

- Give each child a bubble wand. Help each child dip the wand into the bubble solution and then blow bubbles.

SAY: Pretend your bubbles are things you're worried about. You can blow your worries away and trust God to care of you.

Express Praise

Praise and Pray

Supplies: CD-ROM, CD player

- Sing with the children the song "Hear Us As We Pray" from the CD-ROM (lyrics on p. 86). Encourage the children to name any prayer requests.

PRAY: Thank you, God, for taking care of us. Amen.

Blessing

Supplies: child-safe mirror

- Hand one child the mirror. Have the child look into the mirror.

SAY: Thank you, God, for *(child's name)*.

- Continue passing the mirror until you have blessed each child.
- Say the Lord's Prayer together.

Look at the Birds

Everybody who hears these words of mine and puts them into practice is like a wise builder. (Matthew 7:24)

The Golden Rule

Bible Verse: Everybody who hears these words of mine and puts them into practice is like a wise builder. (Matthew 7:24)

Bible Story: Matthew 7:12

biblestorybasics.com

Bible Background

Jesus was raised in the Jewish faith. After the story of his birth, the only story of Jesus' childhood occurs in the temple, where he was found listening to and asking questions of the teachers (Luke 2:41-52). Even when Jesus was young, others were "amazed by his understanding and his answers" (2:47).

When Jesus became an adult and began his teaching ministry, he drew from the religious learning of his younger years. We see evidence of this with what we refer to as the Golden Rule. According to the Talmud, 20 years before Jesus, the rabbi Hillel was challenged by a Gentile to teach the whole law while the Gentile stood on one foot. Hillel replied, "What is hateful to you, do not do to another." Interestingly, similar teachings are found in other faiths as well. When Jesus preached the Golden Rule, he reframed this Jewish teaching in a positive form: "Therefore, you should treat people in the same way that you want people to treat you; this is the Law and the Prophets" (Matthew 7:12). One result of Jesus' reframing of the teaching is that it requires action on our part. It's not enough for us not to treat others badly so that we will not be treated badly. No, we must *do* to others. We must seek out ways to treat others with loving care and compassion, as that is how we would like them to treat us. Living out the Golden Rule requires a conscious effort.

The Golden Rule is short and simple enough for children to memorize it easily. You can help your children realize how this teaching can apply to their lives. Children know how they would like to be treated. This is a great lesson to use to reinforce the message that the words we read in the Bible apply to our lives.

Devotion

The Golden Rule sums up many of Jesus' teachings in Matthew. Jesus said, "You must love your neighbor as you love yourself" (22:39). We want to be loved. Jesus taught that we should feed the hungry, provide drink for the thirsty, welcome the stranger, clothe the naked, and care for the sick (25:35-40). We would like to be cared for by others when we are unable to care for ourselves. Jesus told Peter that he should forgive another not just seven times, but 77 times (18:21-22). We would like others to forgive us. While its application can be complicated and nuanced, Jesus' message is simple and clear.

BASIC

Plan

Bible Beginnings
Welcome
Picture the Bible Story
Bible Puzzle
Bible Play

Into the Bible
Time for the Bible Story
Open the Bible
Experience the Bible Story
Say the Bible Verse

Bible Connections
Gold Collage
Who's Got the Gold?

Live the Bible
Say Nice Words
Make Bookmarks

Express Praise
Praise and Pray
Blessing

Bible Beginnings

Welcome

Supplies: Class Pack—Attendance Chart, p. 6; CD-ROM; CD player; tape; offering basket

- Display the attendance chart (Class Pack) and "Unit 3 Bible Verse Picture" (Class Pack—p. 6) at the children's eye level.
- Play "The B-I-B-L-E" from the CD-ROM (lyrics on p. 85) as you welcome each child.
- Have each child mark his or her attendance.
- Show the children where to place their offerings on the worship table.

SAY: Today, we're going to learn a very important rule. It's so special that we call it the Golden Rule.

- Point out the Bible verse picture, and say the Bible verse for the children.

Picture the Bible Story

Supplies: Leader Guide—p. 78, crayons or markers

- Photocopy "Jesus Teaches the Golden Rule" for each child. Give each child the picture.

SAY: Jesus taught the people a very important rule. It's so special that we call it the Golden Rule. Here's what the Golden Rule says: "Treat people in the same way that you want people to treat you" (Matthew 7:12).

- Encourage the children to decorate the picture with crayons or markers.

Bible Puzzle

Supplies: Bible Story Leaflets—Session 12, p. 4; crayons or markers

- Give each child a copy of today's Bible Story Leaflet.

SAY: Jesus taught the people a very important rule. It's called the Golden Rule because it is so special, like gold.

- Encourage the children to find and circle all the gold things.

Bible Play

Supplies: interlocking blocks or wood blocks

- Encourage the children to build houses with the blocks.

SAY: Our Bible verse is "Everybody who hears these words of mine and puts them into practice is like a wise builder" (Matthew 7:24).

ASK: How do your think a wise builder builds a house? Does the builder build with straw or sticks, like two of the three little pigs? Does the wise builder build with wood and brick?

SAY: Jesus wanted the people to pay attention to the things he was teaching. He wanted the people to be wise.

Into the Bible

Time for the Bible Story

- Sing the following song to the tune of "Do You Know The Muffin Man?" as the children move. End the song in your Story Area.

SING: Do you know this special prayer,
Special prayer, special prayer?
Do you know this special prayer
That Jesus taught his friends?

- Have the children sit down.

SAY: Jesus taught his friends the Lord's Prayer and an important rule. We call this rule the Golden Rule. We can find this rule in the Bible.

Open the Bible

Supplies: Bible Basics Storybook—pp. 150-151

- Tell the children the story "The Golden Rule."

Experience the Bible Story

Supplies: CEB Bible; Bible Story Leaflets—Session 12, pp. 2-3

- Show the children the Bible.

TODAY'S BIBLE TOOL: The teachings of Jesus are in the New Testament.

SAY: Our Bible has many stories. Some of the stories tell about the beginnings of God's people. These stories are in the Old Testament. Some of the stories are about things that Jesus taught us. These stories are in the New Testament.

- Show the children the Book of Matthew. Turn to the seventh chapter of Matthew.

SAY: The very first book in the New Testament is the Book of Matthew. Our Bible story is from the seventh chapter in the Book of Matthew. Listen and watch as I tell the story. You can help me do some sounds and motions.

- Place the leaflet inside the Bible. Tell the children the story "The Golden Rule" from the leaflet, and encourage them to say the words printed in bold and to do the suggested motions with you.

ASK: How do you like to be treated?

Say the Bible Verse

Supplies: Class Pack—p. 6, Leader Guide—p. 89

- Show the children the Bible verse picture (Class Pack). Repeat the verse.
- Teach the children signs in American Sign Language to go along with the verse (Leader Guide).
- Encourage the children to make the signs as they say the verse again.

Bible Connections

Gold Collage

Supplies: Leader Guide—p. 95; scissors; dark construction paper; glue; gold items, such as gold ribbon or rickrack, gold buttons, gold wrapping paper or foil, gold stickers, and small scraps of gold fabric

- Photocopy "The Golden Rule" once for every two children. Cut out a copy of the words of the Golden Rule for each child. (For this activity, each child will only need the words, not the entire rectangle.)

SAY: Jesus taught the people a very important rule. It's called the Golden Rule because it is so special, like gold.

- Give each child a piece of dark construction paper and a copy of the words of the Golden Rule. Have each child glue the words in the middle of his or her paper.
- Encourage each child to glue gold items on the paper around his or her verse.
- Say the Golden Rule with the children.

Who's Got the Gold?

Supplies: unbreakable gold object, such as a gold coin

- Have the children sit on the floor in a circle.

SAY: Today's Bible story teaches an important rule. It's called the Golden Rule because it is so special, like gold.

- Show the children the gold object.
- Choose a child to be "It." Have "It" turn around and cover his or her eyes with his or her hands. Have the rest of the children in the circle hold their hands behind their back. Give one of these children the gold object to hold.
- Have "It" uncover his or her eyes and turn around.

SAY: Gold, gold, who's got the gold? It's your turn to guess who's got the gold.

- Allow "It" three attempts to guess who is holding the gold object. After "It" guesses who is holding the gold object or runs out of attempts, the child holding the object becomes the new "It." Repeat the game as time allows.
- Say the Golden Rule with the children.

Live the Bible

Say Nice Words

Supplies: half sheets of paper, marker, basket

- On separate half sheets of paper, write "Please," "Thank you," "I'm sorry," and "You're welcome." Place the sheets in a basket.

SAY: The Golden Rule teaches us to treat others the way we would like to be treated. One way we can do that is to use nice words when we talk to one another.

- Have the children stand in a circle and hold hands. Place the basket in the middle of the circle, and invite the children to move together in a circle around the basket as they sing the following song to the tune of "Do You Know the Muffin Man?"

SING: Do you know the Golden Rule,
The Golden Rule, the Golden Rule?
Do you know the Golden Rule
That Jesus taught his friends?

- When the song ends, have one child pick a sheet from the basket. Discuss the word or words on the sheet. Talk about when you would use the word or words.
- Continue playing the game until you have discussed all the words.

Make Bookmarks

Supplies: Leader Guide—p. 95, scissors, gold or yellow construction paper, ruler, gold crayons or markers, gold star stickers, glue, hole punch, gold ribbon or yarn

- Photocopy "The Golden Rule" once for every two children. Cut out a rectangle for each child. Cut the construction paper into 3-by-8-inch strips. You will need one strip for each child.
- Give each child a rectangle and strip of construction paper. Encourage each child to decorate the rectangle with gold crayons or markers and gold star stickers.
- Have each child glue the decorated rectangle onto the strip of construction paper to make a bookmark. Punch a hole at the top of each bookmark. Loop a length of gold ribbon or yarn through the hole.
- Say the Golden Rule with the children.

SAY: You can take your bookmark home and place it in your family's Bible to help your family remember the Golden Rule.

Express Praise

Praise and Pray

Supplies: CD-ROM, CD player

- Sing with the children the song "Hear Us As We Pray" from the CD-ROM (lyrics on p. 86). Encourage the children to name any prayer requests.

PRAY: Thank you, God, for the Golden Rule. Help us treat others the way we want to be treated. Amen.

Blessing

Supplies: child-safe mirror

- Hand one child the mirror. Have the child look into the mirror.

SAY: Thank you, God, for *(child's name)*.

- Continue passing the mirror until you have blessed each child.
- Say the Lord's Prayer together.

Jesus Teaches the Golden Rule

Treat people in the same way that you want people to treat you.

Everybody who hears these words of mine and puts them into practice is like a wise builder. (Matthew 7:24)

The Two Houses

Bible Verse: Everybody who hears these words of mine and puts them into practice is like a wise builder. (Matthew 7:24)

Bible Story: Matthew 7:24-27

biblestorybasics.com

Bible Background

Jesus often used stories when he was teaching. Many of the stories Jesus told are parables—stories specifically used to teach a lesson. Occasionally, Jesus would explain the meaning of the parables he told to his disciples. More often, Jesus told these stories without explanation. The work of figuring out what Jesus meant was left to us. Some of Jesus' stories are challenging to understand, particularly reading them many years outside of the context in which they were told, as we are. Perhaps this was one of the reasons Jesus taught in parables: so that his followers would continue to ask questions.

The parable of the wise and foolish builders is presented in Matthew as part of Jesus' Sermon on the Mount. The story is in a similar form in the Gospel of Luke. Jesus spoke of two builders who each built a house. One builder built his house on rock, and the other builder built his house on sand. And then the rains came. Those originally listening to Jesus' story were familiar with wadis, desert areas that are usually dry but flood in the rainy season. Houses built on the sand in these areas would last only until the heavy rains flooded the area.

Jesus explained this parable by comparing those who hear his words and follow them to the wise builder. Those who hear Jesus' teachings and ignore them were likened to the foolish builder. Everyone who hears Jesus' teachings has the same knowledge. Each person makes a choice about how to use that knowledge.

Devotion

In this parable, Jesus cautioned us to take care how we build our lives. He told us to make God our foundation. There are many Scriptures that use imagery of God as our foundation, the rock on which we may build our lives. Read Psalm 62:2 and Psalm 95:1. How do these ancient hymns make you feel? Say a prayer thanking God for giving you a sure foundation.

BASIC

Plan

Bible Beginnings
Welcome
Picture the Bible Story
Bible Puzzle
Bible Play

Into the Bible
Time for the Bible Story
Open the Bible
Experience the Bible Story
Say the Bible Verse

Bible Connections
Make Houses
Sing the Story

Live the Bible
Experiment with the Story
Review Jesus' Teachings

Express Praise
Praise and Pray
Blessing

Bible Beginnings

Welcome

Supplies: Class Pack—Attendance Chart, p. 6; CD-ROM; CD player; tape; offering basket

- Display the attendance chart (Class Pack) and "Unit 3 Bible Verse Picture" (Class Pack—p. 6) at the children's eye level.
- Play "The B-I-B-L-E" from the CD-ROM (lyrics on p. 85) as you welcome each child.
- Have each child mark his or her attendance.
- Show the children where to place their offerings on the worship table.

SAY: Today, our Bible story is a story Jesus told about two houses.

- Point out the Bible verse picture, and say the Bible verse for the children.

Picture the Bible Story

Supplies: Leader Guide—p. 84, crayons or markers

- Photocopy "The Two Houses" for each child. Give each child the picture.

SAY: Today, our Bible story is a story Jesus told about two houses. A wise builder built his house on rock. A foolish builder built his house on sand.

- Encourage the children to decorate the picture with crayons or markers.

ASK: Why do you think it was wise to build on rock? What do you think might have happened to the house built on the sand?

Bible Puzzle

Supplies: Bible Story Leaflets—Session 13, p. 4; crayons or markers

- Give each child a copy of today's Bible Story Leaflet.

SAY: Jesus told a story about two houses. A wise builder built his house on rock. A foolish builder built his house on sand.

- Encourage the children to circle the five differences between the two houses.

Bible Play

Supplies: interlocking blocks or wood blocks

- Encourage the children to build houses with the blocks.

SAY: Our Bible verse is "Everybody who hears these words of mine and puts them into practice is like a wise builder" (Matthew 7:24).

ASK: How do your think a wise builder builds a house? Does the builder build with straw or sticks, like two of the three little pigs? Does the wise builder build with wood and brick?

SAY: Jesus wanted the people to pay attention to the things he was teaching. He wanted the people to be wise.

Into the Bible

Time for the Bible Story

- Sing the following song to the tune of "Do You Know The Muffin Man?" as the children move. End the song in your Story Area.

SING: Do you know this special prayer,
Special prayer, special prayer?
Do you know this special prayer
That Jesus taught his friends?

- Have the children sit down.

SAY: Jesus taught the Lord's Prayer and told stories called parables to help people know how God wants us to live. Today, we'll hear a parable about a wise builder who built a house on rock and a foolish builder who built a house on sand.

Open the Bible

Supplies: Bible Basics Storybook—pp. 152-153

- Tell the children the story "The Two Houses."

Experience the Bible Story

Supplies: CEB Bible; Bible Story Leaflets—Session 13, pp. 2-3

- Show the children the Bible.

TODAY'S BIBLE TOOL: The teachings of Jesus are in the New Testament.

SAY: Our Bible has many stories. Some of the stories tell about the beginnings of God's people. These stories are in the Old Testament. Some of the stories are about things that Jesus taught us. These stories are in the New Testament.

- Show the children the Book of Matthew. Turn to the seventh chapter of Matthew.

SAY: The very first book in the New Testament is the Book of Matthew. Our Bible story is from the seventh chapter in the Book of Matthew. Listen and watch as I tell the story. You can help me do some sounds and motions.

- Place the leaflet inside the Bible. Tell the children the story "The Two Houses" from the leaflet, and encourage them to say the word printed in bold and to do the suggested motions with you.

SAY: The wise builder built his house on rock. The foolish builder built his house on sand.

Say the Bible Verse

Supplies: Class Pack—p. 6, Leader Guide—p. 89

- Show the children the Bible verse picture (Class Pack). Repeat the verse.
- Teach the children signs in American Sign Language to go along with the verse (Leader Guide).
- Encourage the children to make the signs as they say the verse again.

Bible Connections

Make Houses

Supplies: construction paper, crayons or markers, glue, craft sticks

SAY: Our Bible story is a story Jesus told about two houses. Jesus said that the wise man built his house with rock for a foundation. Let's make a picture of that house.

- Give each child a piece of construction paper. Let the children use crayons or marker to make ground or dirt at the bottom of their paper.

SAY: The wise man built his house with rock for a foundation. Let's make good foundations for our houses.

- Give each child three craft sticks. Show the children how to glue the craft sticks horizontally in a row across the bottom of their paper.

SAY: Now we're ready to finish the houses.

- Give the children more craft sticks. Let the children glue these craft sticks in the shape of a house above their foundation sticks.

Sing the Story

Supplies: none

SAY: Our Bible story is a story Jesus told about two houses. The wise builder built his house on rock. The foolish man built his house on sand. Let's sing the story.

- Sing the following action poem to the tune of "The Wise Man and the Foolish Man," and lead the children in doing the motions.

The wise man built his house upon the rock.
(Tap one fist on top of the other fist.)
The wise man built his house upon the rock.
The wise man built his house upon the rock.
And the rains came tumbling down.
(Hold up your hands, and then bring your hands down while wiggling your fingers.)
The rains came down, and the floods came up.
(Turn your palms upward, and then move your hands up.)
The rains came down, and the floods came up.
The rains came down, and the floods came up.
But the house on the rock stood firm.
(Tap one fist on top of the other fist.)

The foolish man built his house upon the sand.
(Tap the fist of one hand on the palm of the other hand.)
The foolish man built his house upon the sand.
The foolish man built his house upon the sand.
And the rains came tumbling down.
(Hold up your hands, and then bring your hands down while wiggling your fingers.)
The rains came down, and the floods came up.
(Turn your palms upward, and then move your hands up.)
The rains came down, and the floods came up.
The rains came down, and the floods came up.
And the house on the sand fell flat.
(Slap your hands together.)

Live the Bible

Experiment with the Story

Supplies: small plastic tub or cake pan, sand, sponge, pitcher of water, one flat rock

- Place a layer of sand in the bottom of the tub or pan.

SAY: Let's pretend this sponge is a house. Let's see what happens when we build the house on sand.

- Place the sponge on the sand. Pour water over the sand.

ASK: What happened to our house?

SAY: When it rained, the house built on sand fell down.

- Remove the sand from the tub or pan, and place the flat rock in the bottom of the tub or pan. Place the sponge on the rock. Pour water in the bottom of the tub or pan.

SAY: The house built on rock stood firm.

Review Jesus' Teachings

Supplies: none

- Have the children sit down in an open area of the room.

SAY: We've learned some things Jesus taught. If Jesus taught what I say, jump up and shout, "I can do it!" If it's not something Jesus taught, stay seated.

SAY: Jesus taught the Lord's Prayer *(Jump and shout.)*, the happy dance *(Stay seated.)*, the silver rule *(Stay seated.)*, the Golden Rule *(Jump and shout.)*, that we should worry *(Stay seated.)*, that we don't need to worry. *(Jump and shout.)*

Express Praise

Praise and Pray

Supplies: CD-ROM, CD player

- Sing with the children the song "Hear Us As We Pray" from the CD-ROM (lyrics on p. 86). Encourage the children to name any prayer requests.

PRAY: Thank you, God, for all the things Jesus taught us. Amen.

Blessing

Supplies: child-safe mirror

- Hand one child the mirror. Have the child look into the mirror.

SAY: Thank you, God, for *(child's name)*.

- Continue passing the mirror until you have blessed each child.
- Say the Lord's Prayer together.

The Two Houses

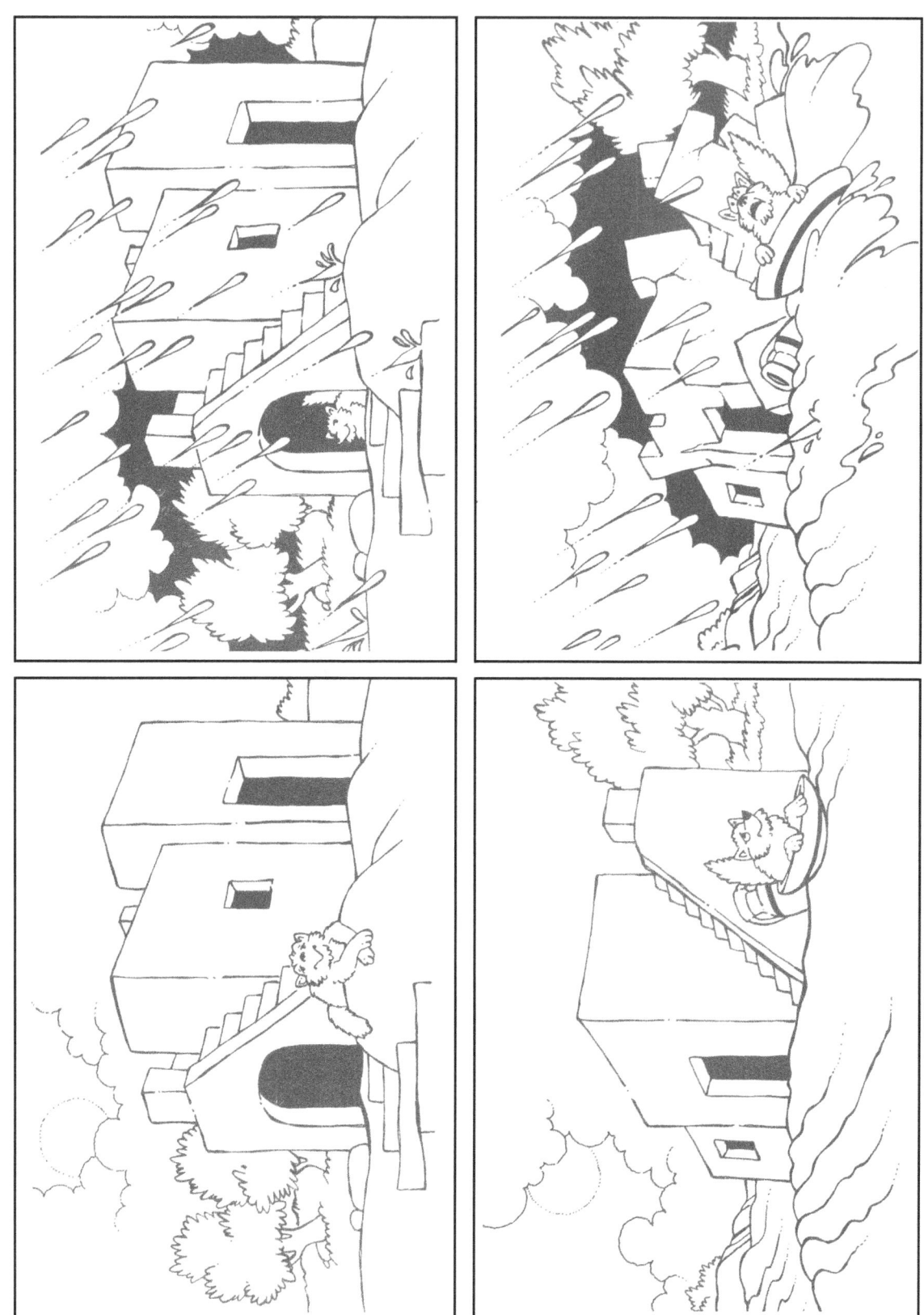

Everybody who hears these words of mine and puts them into practice is like a wise builder. (Matthew 7:24)

The B-I-B-L-E
Theme Song

The B-I-B-L-E
Yes, that's the book for me.
I stand alone on the Word of God.
The B-I-B-L-E

B-I-B-L-E (4x)

It starts in Genesis with the Creation
And ends when Jesus returns in Revelation.
And in between the greatest story ever told,
Of Jesus' love for you and me that never lets us go.

Open up the Word, and you'll see
God's plan for you and me.

The B-I-B-L-E, B-I-B-L-E
I stand alone on the Word of God.
The B-I-B-L-E
The B-I-B-L-E, B-I-B-L-E
I stand alone on the Word of God.
The B-I-B-L-E

For every tongue and tribe, for every nation,
It's the gospel of the one who brings salvation.
And one day every knee will bow before the throne.
Until then we've been given everything we need to know.

Open up the Word, and you'll see
God's plan for you and me.

The B-I-B-L-E, B-I-B-L-E
I stand alone on the Word of God.
The B-I-B-L-E
The B-I-B-L-E, B-I-B-L-E
I stand alone on the Word of God.
The B-I-B-L-E

Let's get back to the basics, back to the word,
Back to the greatest news the world's ever heard.
Back to the basics, back to the word,
Back to the greatest news the world's ever heard.

B-I-B-I-B-L-E

The B-I-B-L E, B-I-B-L-E
I stand alone on the Word of God.
The B-I-B-L-E
The B-I-B-L-E, B-I-B-L-E
I stand alone on the Word of God.
The B-I-B-L-E

Words: Andrew Wilson
Music: Andrew Wilson

© 2019 Andrew Wilson. Used by permission. All rights reserved.

Hear Us As We Pray
Prayer Song

Lord, we call to you right now.
Hear us as we pray.

Folded hands and quiet hearts
Hear us as we pray.

Give us heroes' hearts.
Reveal your truth today.
Give us strength to do what's good.
Hear us as we pray.
Hear us as we pray.

Lord, we ask this in your name.
Hear us as we pray.

Boldly share, your truth proclaim.
Hear us as we pray.

Give us heroes' hearts
To live your truth each day.
Give us courage in our faith.
Hear us as we pray.
Hear us as we pray.

Lord, we call to you right now.
Hear us as we pray.

Guide our feet and light our way.
Hear us as we pray.

Give us heroes' hearts
In all we do and say.
Give us hope as we seek peace.
Hear us as we pray.
Hear us as we pray.

Hear us as we pray.

Words: Matt Huesmann
Music: Matt Huesmann

© 2017 Matt Huesmann Music. Used by permission. All rights reserved.

Isaiah 2:5

Unit 1 Bible Verse Signs

Let's **walk** by the Lord's **light**.

Walk

Hold both of your hands in front of your body. Move your hands up and down.

Lord

Hold your right index finger and right thumb in an L shape. Place the L on your left shoulder, and then move the L across your body to your right waist.

Light

Hold your right hand at eye level. Flick all five fingers down and out.

Matthew 4:19

Unit 2 Bible Verse Signs

Come, follow me.

Come

Point your right index finger away from yourself, and then point the finger at yourself.

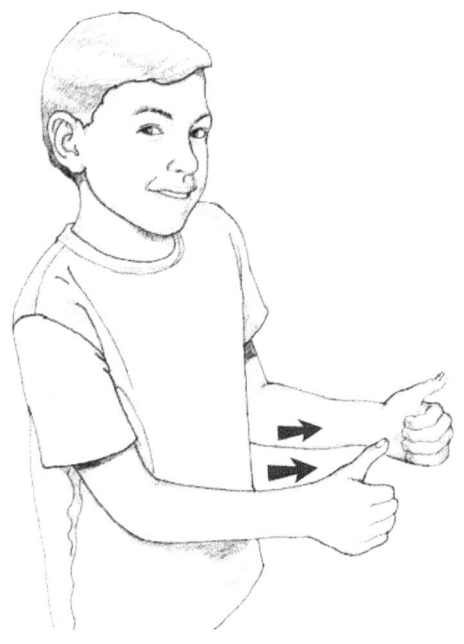

Follow

Make fists with both hands, and stick your thumbs up from the fists. Hold your hands in front of your body, with your right hand slightly behind your left hand. Move both hands forward.

Me

Point your right index finger at yourself.

Matthew 7:24

Unit 3 Bible Verse Signs

Everybody who **hears** these words of mine and puts them into **practice** is like a **wise builder**.

Everybody

Make a fist with your right hand, and stick your thumb up from the fist. Touch your chest with your right thumb, and then point your right index finger upward and circle your right hand in front of your body.

Hears

Point your right index finger at your right ear.

Practice

Hold your right hand in a fist, and stick your thumb out from the fist. Hold your left hand sideways, with your left thumb tucked and your left index finger at the top. Rub your right wrist back and forth quickly across your left index finger.

  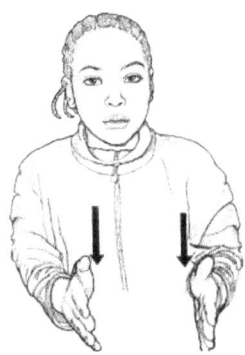

Wise

Crook your right index finger. Move the finger up and down at the right side of your forehead.

Then add the sign for *person*. Hold both hands parallel, with your palms facing each other. Move both hands down.

Builder

Bend your hands, and hold your fingers together. Hold your hands in front of your body, with your right hand on top of your left hand. Move your left hand up, and place it on top of your right hand. Alternate moving each hand up and placing it on top of the other hand.

Then add the sign for *person*. Hold both hands parallel, with your palms facing each other. Move both hands down.

Permission is granted to duplicate this page for local church use only. © 2019 Abingdon Press.

Scroll Ornaments
Session 1—pp. 10, 11

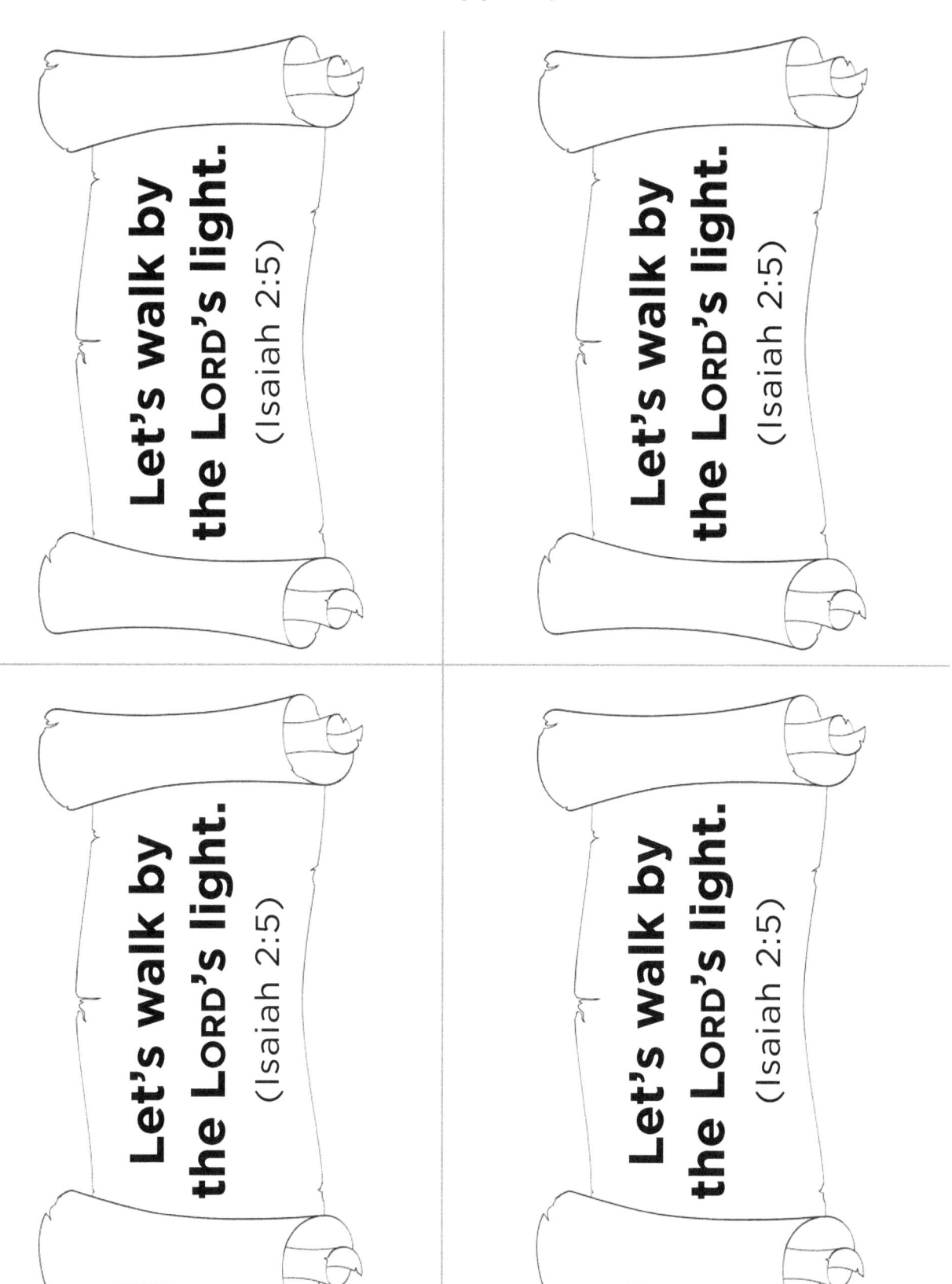

Permission is granted to duplicate this page for local church use only. © 2019 Abingdon Press.

Star Poles

Session 6—p. 40

Happiness Jar

Session 7—pp. 46, 47

God loves you.
God finds happiness in you.
You make me smile.
I like being with you.
You are special to me.
I'm glad you're part of our family.
I love you.

Invite a Friend
Session 8—p. 53

Come, follow me to...

... learn about Jesus.

The Lord's Prayer
Session 10—p. 64

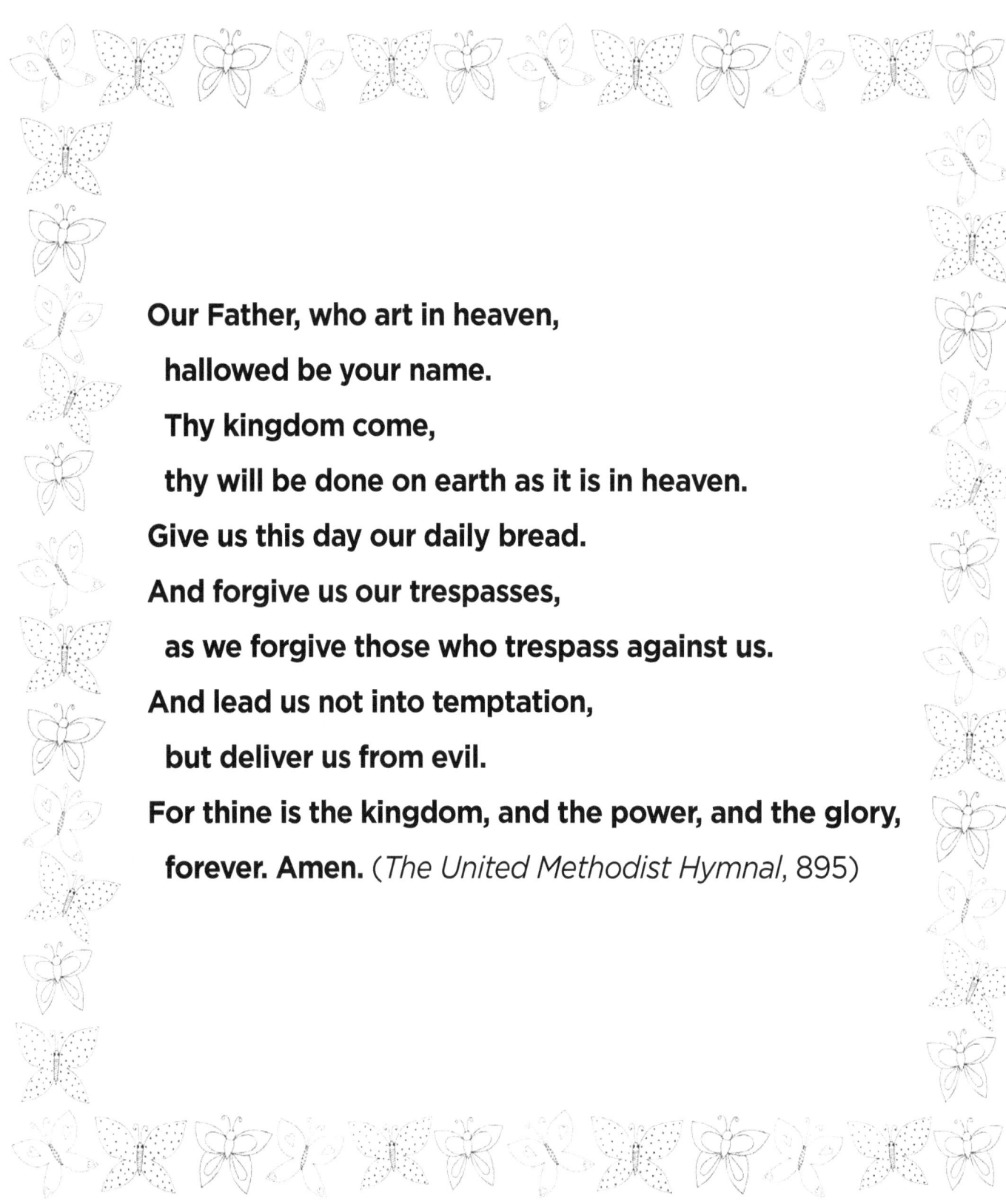

Our Father, who art in heaven,
  hallowed be your name.
  Thy kingdom come,
  thy will be done on earth as it is in heaven.
Give us this day our daily bread.
And forgive us our trespasses,
  as we forgive those who trespass against us.
And lead us not into temptation,
  but deliver us from evil.
For thine is the kingdom, and the power, and the glory,
  forever. Amen. *(The United Methodist Hymnal, 895)*

The Golden Rule

Session 12—pp. 76, 77

Treat people
in the same way
that you want people
to treat you.

Matthew 7:12

Treat people
in the same way
that you want people
to treat you.

Matthew 7:12

Comments from Users

Let us know what you think! Your comments will help us write a better curriculum for you and the children you teach. Please send your comments and suggestions to:

Daphna Flegal, Children's Unit
The United Methodist Publishing House
2222 Rosa L. Parks Blvd.
Nashville, TN 37228-1306

Please check the components that you use:

_____ Leader Guide
_____ Bible Story Leaflets
_____ Class Pack
_____ Student Take-Home CD
_____ Bible Basics Storybook

Use the following scale to rate each of the resources:
N/A = Not Applicable
1 = Never
2 = Sometimes
3 = Most of the Time
4 = All of the Time

Leader Guide

_____ The Leader Guide was easy to use.
_____ Children grew to understand the Bible stories from the suggested activities.

Comments about Leader Guide:
_____
_____
_____

Bible Story Leaflets

_____ The children enjoyed moving to the Bible stories as they were read to them.

Comments about Bible Story Leaflets:
_____
_____
_____

Class Pack

_____ The Bible verse pictures were colorful and engaging for the children.
_____ We used the attendance chart.

Student Take-Home CD

_____ The children enjoyed learning and singing the songs on the CD.

Bible Basics Storybook

_____ The children enjoyed hearing the retellings of the Bible stories.

My favorite activity this quarter was _____
_____
_____

My least favorite activity this quarter was _____
_____
_____

Overall, I would rate this **Winter 2019-20** quarter: _____

3 = The best that it could possibly be.
2 = Provided some good moments for the children's faith development.
1 = Ineffective with the faith development of the children in my church.

Leader's Name: _____
Church: _____
Address: _____
_____
_____
Phone No.: _____

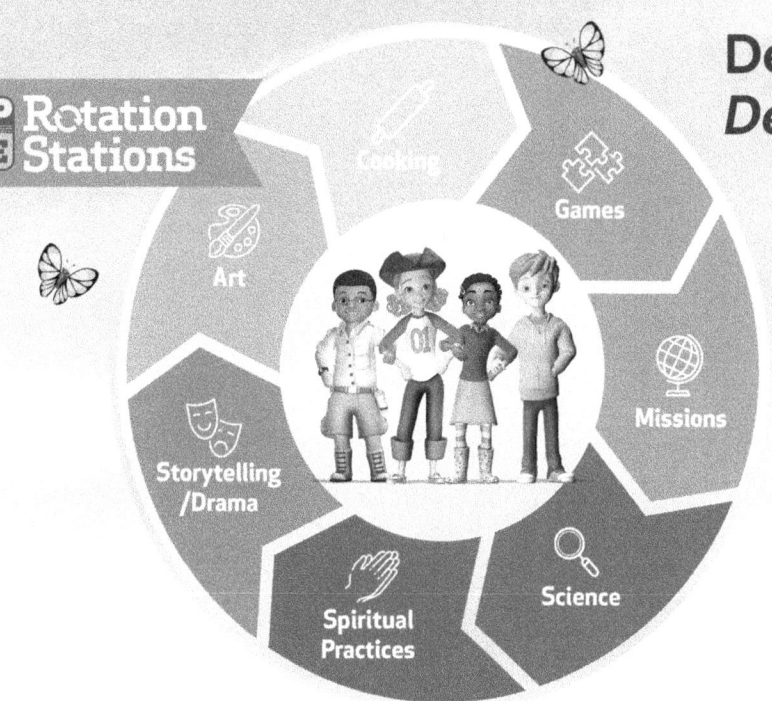

Deepen learning with *Deep Blue Rotation Stations*!

As children visit a different learning station each week, they'll explore the Bible story from multiple angles for deeper, more engaged learning. Perfect for busy volunteers—plan one lesson, then teach it to different age groups over several weeks. Numerous topics available in full 7-week units, or choose individual stations for a shorter rotation. Perfect for midweek! Grades K–5.

For a complete list of units and individual station downloads, see Cokesbury.com or go to deepbluekids.com/rotation.

800-672-1789 | Cokesbury.com
Call a Resource Consultant

Winter Year 1
Vol. 1 • No. 2

BIBLE STORY BASICS: PRE-READER, LEADER GUIDE: An official resource for The United Methodist Church approved by Discipleship Ministries and published quarterly by Abingdon Press, a division of The United Methodist Publishing House, 2222 Rosa L. Parks Blvd., Nashville, TN 37228-1306. Price: $14.99. Copyright © 2019 Abingdon Press. All rights reserved. Send address changes to BIBLE STORY BASICS: PRE-READER, LEADER GUIDE, Subscription Services, 2222 Rosa L. Parks Blvd., Nashville, TN 37228-1306 or call 800-672-1789. Printed in the United States of America.

To order copies of this publication, call toll free: **800-672-1789**. You may fax your order to 800-445-8189. Telecommunication Device for the Deaf/Telex Telephone: 800-227-4091. Or order online at *cokesbury.com*. Use your Cokesbury account, American Express, Visa, Discover, or Mastercard.

For information concerning permission to reproduce any material in this publication, write to Rights and Permissions, The United Methodist Publishing House, 2222 Rosa L. Parks Blvd., Nashville, TN 37228-1306. You may fax your request to 615-749-6128. Or email *permissions@umpublishing.org*.

Scripture quotations are taken from the Common English Bible, copyright 2011. Used by permission. All rights reserved.

PACP10557323-01

EDITORIAL / DESIGN TEAM
Daphna Flegal . . . . Writer/Editor
Lucas Hilliard . . . . Production Editor
Jim Carlton . . . . Designer

ADMINISTRATIVE TEAM
Rev. Brian K. Milford . . . . President and Publisher
Marjorie M. Pon . . . . Associate Publisher and Editor of Church School Publications (CSP)
Mary M. Mitchell . . . . Design Manager
Brittany Sky . . . . Senior Editor, Children's Resources

www.ingramcontent.com/pod-product-compliance
Lightning Source LLC
LaVergne TN
LVHW061315060426
835507LV00019B/2158